A Philosophy of Church Music

A Philosophy
of Church Music

by
Robert D. Berglund

MOODY PRESS
CHICAGO

© 1985 by
ROBERT D. BERGLUND

Library of Congress Cataloging-in-Publication Data

Berglund, Robert D., 1930–
  A philosophy of church music.

  Bibliography: p.
  1. Church music.   2. Music—Philosophy and aesthetics.   I. Title.
  ML3869.B37   1985   783′.02′6   85-13695
  ISBN 0-8024-0279-8

2 3 4 5 6 7 Printing/AF/Year 89 88 87

Printed in the United States of America

In grateful appreciation to a mother and father whose lives have always reflected the most noble of intentions in an integration of scriptural values and all of life as it is lived for my Savior and others;

To my loving children, Jackie and John, and my devoted wife, Margaret, who have always been encouraging, positive in criticism, and supportive in my church music ministries; and

To Pastor Paul M. Youngdahl, Senior Pastor of Mount Olivet Lutheran Church, and all other faithful pastors who preach the gospel and are keenly aware and supportive of a decisive and comprehensive ministry of music in the church of Christ, I dedicate these pages to the glory of God.

The hour cometh, and now is, when the true worshippers shall worship the Father in spirit and in truth: for the Father seeketh such to worship him.

God is a Spirit: and they that worship him must worship him in spirit and in truth.

(John 4:23–24)

Contents

Preface

Church music, like many other aspects of modern life, has in recent years undergone changes and shifts due in part to the changing times. Some of the changes have been long overdue and are the result of well thought-out planning by church musicians and pastors. Resistance to much-needed change by some is often the result of personal insecurity regarding church music philosophy. Resistance can also be attributed to church leadership that is sometimes ineffective in preparing for and leading in new and constructive directions. Change that results from careful analysis of need within the context of agreed-upon philosophical and theological presuppositions is healthy. However, change "for the sake of change" or change resulting from naive church pressure groups is hardly desirable.

Few churches have been untouched in recent years by at least some winds of change that have resulted in dissension within the congregation. All too often, some of that change has come about through musicians' and pastors' efforts that were ill-founded and contradictory to their own professed theological or philosophical tenets. More often than not, plausible ends (such as keeping the young people coming to church) gave credence to a means that was seriously lacking in the spiritual essence that the church professed to desire for its young people. That problem can often be attributed to two knowledge-based causes.

- The musicians have often been well educated in the craft and art of music (they sing or play the piano or organ well) but have had little understanding in the theological and philosophical framework essential for providing stability and consistent direction.
- The pastors have been well educated theologically and philosophically but often have had little or no understanding in the art of music and its application to church music.

Most books in church music have tended to be primarily either historic, philosophic, or of the how-to type. It is my intent to here provide the church musician, pastor, layperson, and the student of church music with an integrated synthesis of theological, philosophical, and psychological considerations in addition to some practical procedures that may be helpful in the evaluative process, thereby assisting in the development of a personal church music philosophy that is both consistent and practical.

PART 1
THE PROCESSES OF CHURCH MUSIC

1

Music and the Word

THE BEGINNING STEP IN THE PROCESS DEVELOPMENT

When endeavoring to develop a unifying philosophic system based upon biblical principles, it becomes necessary to internalize those principles from Scripture that apply to any given situation. A practical understanding of the Word of God should be basic to any believer's decision-making process. To imply that an awareness of the utilization of music in twenty or thirty scriptural instances would provide all the answers to current questions is, however, absurdly naive. Conversely, the notion that complex biblical principles interact in such a way so as to be either contradictory or inadequate for our times is, in my opinion, a "cop-out." No serious student today suggests a proof-texting approach as the answer to current questions. A mere dipping into isolated portions of the Word for answers is therefore not at all what is advocated here. Rather, a systematic study of the Word becomes essential to not only understand conditions surrounding the utilization of music within given contexts, but also to develop a sensitivity to the basic principles of the Word that are applicable to music situations as well as to other areas of life. That is not a one-shot or short-term educational pursuit. It is a life-long process that needs to be pursued with commitment and Holy Spirit directed zeal. To assume that a person can effectively minister through music if he is only prepared as a musician is a gross misunderstanding of the nature of *ministering through music*. A casual acquaintance with biblical truth is inadequate. The challenge is to require of oneself a growing awareness of the Word so that daily decisions are made within the wholistic context of the Word.

THE SEARCH FOR AND APPLICATION OF TRUTH

Undoubtedly, one should endeavor to understand various philosophic positions in order to better understand differing points of view. That would enable one to share scriptural truth at a higher level and, potentially, be more effective. The questions might arise, "Are there not differing points of view in attempting to arrive at spiritual truth? Do not theologians themselves differ as to what the premises are and what truth is?" The answers, of course, are yes. There are differing opinions. But ultimately there is no reason why one should not seek both revelational and empirical truth.* It is one's responsibility then to discover the truth for oneself; truth not only arrived at through reasoning abilities and the best research of scholars but through the guidance of the Holy Spirit as well. Scripture suggests there is only *one truth* and that truth is made available to man through the guidance of the Spirit. John 16:13 (which speaks of the work of the Holy Spirit) states: "Howbeit when he, the Spirit of truth, is come, he will guide you into all truth."

Perhaps one of the most insidious works of Satan today is to create an indifference towards the pursuit of truth. Some Christians may say, "Why try to arrive at truth from Scripture? There are so many differing ideas about it—it's a waste of time for me. Who am I that I might arrive at truth when the great theologians cannot agree?" That rationalization often causes some never to seriously come to grips with the Word, and Satan has been successful in circumventing the believer around one of the most important elements of the Christian life, an awareness of spiritual truth.

Is it any wonder, then, that some elements of philosophic relativism, which in some aspects is at odds with Scripture, are not uncommon among Christians? Second Timothy 2:15 instructs Christians to "study, . . . rightly dividing [properly applying] the word of truth." It is thus apparent that one must know the truth of the Word in order to be an effective Christian as well as an effective church music leader. One

---

Revelational truth is the arena of knowledge verifiable by experience but not by scientific method (i.e., a believer's faith). Empirical truth is the arena of knowledge verifiable by scientific method.

must be well equipped with the understanding and application of basic scriptural truth. In the peripheral areas where there is room for varying opinions it is also important to refrain from dogmatism. The problem is that often those who concur with the value of seeking truth fall into the trap of thinking that only they have the truth. Such closed positions reflect a lack of scholarship and/or a theological inferiority complex. What is here advocated is an openness to divergent opinions where there is lack of evidence, but strength of conviction in basic areas that are soundly supported by evidence. Tolerance may reflect breadth of understanding or no understanding at all. Put another way, in the basics of life, church musicians should be solid and unswerving.

How does one achieve that kind of facility in Scripture? In some ways the answer seems obvious, yet in others it is elusive. The following is what I personally believe to be the path to such facility.

- Of primary importance is that the individual has a vital faith in Jesus Christ as Savior and Lord. One must have experienced the miracle of saving grace as a prerequisite, but one must also submit to the lordship of Christ in order to further the total transaction of regeneration.
- One must make a concerted effort to develop a biblically sound value system.
- One must integrate the values of the Word with the best values of music training.

Of course it is possible that some who profess to be Christians may not in fact be Christians. If there is a serious difference between what Scripture defines as Christianity and what exists in the lives of people who claim to be Christians, either the scriptural definition is wrong or the claimants are wrong. Assuming Scripture to be correct, a person's behavior will either support or betray his commitment.

In summary then, the Christian musician must be well equipped in the understanding and application of basic scriptural truth. Personal study, courses in Christian colleges or seminaries, and church music workshops can all help the musician to arrive at that ideal. It is unthinkable that a church musician should only be qualified as a musician. It is more reasonable that he be equally qualified in his spiritual perceptions as well.

2

Church Music Values

Church musicians are called upon to function in many different roles. Usual responsibilities may include planning and administering a complete music program, directing the choir or choirs, playing the organ for services, and educating congregations in the relationships that exist between the art of music and scripturally based texts. One of the factors that separates church music from non-church music is its involvement of scriptural truth and principles. (Other factors are discussed later.) The role of Scripture in church music makes it apparent that much of what church musicians do is not only in the role of conductor or performer but is to a very great extent also in the realm of decision making, philosophy formation, and ideology execution. Church musicians are called upon to advise individuals and ensembles in the literature they perform, to evaluate and select those musical selections that are worthy of performance, and, in general, to make frequent judgments concerning the total program. That process requires a considerable understanding on the musician's part. If all he had to do was conduct, how easy the task would be! But all church musicians are thrust into decision-making areas that often become their primary responsibilities.

One's *decisions* are usually based upon one's *values*, that is, the actual values one has determine the kinds of decisions one makes. There is sometimes a gap between verbalized values and actual behavior. Behavior inconsistent with verbalized values simply reflects *actual* values different from *verbalized* values. I am personally convinced that the field of axiology—the study of values—is one area in which church musicians are often non-conversant. Their education adequately prepares them to be good performers, but whatever strengths exist in the development of sound philosophical value systems have been arrived at by chance. The importance of the roles of policy-maker, decision-maker, or leader in the total realm of church music is too great to allow those roles to be guided by poorly thought-out systems. Forgetting temporarily one's strengths or limitations in conducting mixed meters or playing in B major, attention will here be focused upon the values that cause one to believe what one believes, decide what one decides, and ultimately do what one does. Consider with me *your* church music value system.

This is a day when both constructive and destructive ideologies are plentiful. Change is the norm, and the world seems to be exploding at the seams. On the one hand, problems of war, pollution, drugs, poverty, taxes, immorality, and population growth seem insurmountable. On the other hand, man doubles the knowledge base every decade rather than every 150 to 300 years, and the mass media have made the propagation of the gospel to the entire world a reality. Nations in Africa and South America are experiencing revivals that stagger the imagination, to say nothing of the miraculous stories of God's working in mainland China and Russia. In spite of the problems of the world, standards of living have improved to a marked degree. This is an age when things are happening so fast it is virtually impossible to keep pace. And yet, for a person to be an effective minister of Christ, he must also be effective in his evaluations and appraisals of world situations as well as keep abreast of the rapid changes. Thoughtfulness in those evaluative procedures may lead to more effective personal judgments, including those judgments involving church music. Generally, the person who is totally negative towards the world and its course is "tuned out" by the world because he is perceived as anti-world. Regardless of the degree of truth he has, his negativism renders him ineffective in meeting his goals. On the other hand, the habitual optimist who sees only through rose-colored glasses is so idealistic that he is out of touch with reality. There must be a point between the two extremes that would enable one to possess the best of both positions.

GOD'S VALUE SYSTEM

As God viewed man, He saw man as the sinful, helpless creature that he is, but He also saw man with a potential for good—having been originally created in His image.* Therefore, God's judgmental requirements were balanced with His love—a love that provided the possibility of escape from the sentence demanded by the law. God's view of man, then, is judgmental, strict, precise, and in fact, completely authoritative. However, through man's acceptance of the saving grace of Christ, God sees man not only from His role as Judge but also as Father, for man is born into the family of God, and his true potential for spirituality is established. Man's sinful nature is replaced with the potential for a God-directed spiritual nature. Scripture expresses this metamorphosis aptly in many verses including the familiar "For God so loved the world, that he gave his only begotten Son, that whosoever believeth in him should not perish, but have everlasting life" (John 3:16). Scripture is replete with examples of God's modus operandi. John 3:16 delineates how God operates in His process of making judgments. It indicates the kind of *system* of values He has, and it thereby can assist in the development of one's own value systems. Note that God loves, yet His just nature demands a payment for sins. That suggests a process not of chance but of careful, thoughtful action. God's decision-making process is not a haphazard one. Christians need to follow His example and make sound evaluations of situations in order to be effective in relating the message of the gospel to the world.

God's value system is cohesive, unified, and perfectly planned; Christians also need to be thoughtful in the development of their own value systems. The basis for an effective system is not blanket negativism or blind positivism but evaluations based upon biblical principles that apply to current needs. Most church musicians can wax eloquent on the problems or strengths of current trends in church music; but many times the reasoning is merely man's intellectual prowess with its attendant strengths and weaknesses. In evaluating the state of church music, one should strive not only to do so on the basis of professional expertise but also on the basis of the underlying principles of the Word of God. It is possible to experience a moral victory in philosophical debates won because of musical awareness and yet see no behavioral change in the conquered. Although intellectual ascent has been won, the truth of the point has not been accepted at the behavioral level; thus no change is evoked. On the other hand, where the Spirit of God

*See pages 18–21 concerning this fact as it relates to aesthetics.

is present through the power of God's Word, such debates no longer contain the "convincing" arguments of man but the life-changing, behavior-changing power of God. I have met many effective church musicians and pastors who have not had the privilege of an extended formal education in the areas of philosophy and/or theology. I have been aware of their inadequacies in formulating logical arguments against questionable practices. However, they have had an intuition or perhaps the leading of the Spirit of God Himself and have been able to determine whether or not a practice was in keeping with their basic desire to have a Christ-centered ministry. Unquestionably it is essential that the Christian be expert in his chosen field—whether or not that involves formal training. There is little room for mediocrity in church musicians, pastors, bankers, teachers, or in any other vocation. God deserves the finest man can produce. However, the Christian must give ultimate allegiance to the truth of the Word of God and be an expert in rightly dividing that truth. Evaluations of situations will then be permeated by a sensitivity to other viewpoints in Christian love, yet the principles drawn from Scripture will carry the greatest weight in all areas. An integrative process will take place between the values of God's Word and the values of one's profession. It is not surprising that the Spirit can better evoke changes in responses than can man's best reasoning and debative techniques. *To develop a practical working value system it is important that church musicians be qualified in both the Word of God and the discipline of music.* For church musicians, that means thorough preparation as conductors, instrumentalists, or singers. As a matter of fact, because of one's basic understanding of and obedience to the Word, careful attention should be given to the development of abilities and talents to the fullest. In addition, one must be pragmatically prepared in the teachings of the Word as well. If that is accomplished, one's value systems will be properly based and in accord with God's value system.

APPLICATION: A VALUE SYSTEM FOR A CHURCH MUSICIAN

Normally this discussion would end at the above point. Frequently, the observation is made by pastors, teachers, and others that they agree with principles yet find it difficult to put the kind of reasoning necessary into everyday action. Rather than end with a general appeal to "do better," the discussion will now become more specific with an example of how to start developing a value system in the area of church music.

One must always be careful so as to not simply extract a verse from Scripture to prove a point. Ridiculous assertions can be made by *proof-*

texting, and that approach is certainly not here advocated. However, Scripture is intended to provide daily guidance through principles that are well-established, not only in a single verse but in complete chapters and books. By internalizing those principles, direction that involves both correction and reinforcement can be found. One should not fear internalizing biblical principles because one disagrees with the proof-texting approach. Care must simply be taken to be sure that principles are not isolated or extracted in self-serving models to reinforce personal bias or ideas. The principle found in 2 Corinthians 5:17 will be used to illustrate a proper approach. This verse states:

> Therefore, if any man be in Christ, he is a new creature; old things are passed away; behold, all things are become new.

THE PRINCIPLE

The principle of this verse is clearly stated: *man is changed radically* if man is in fact regenerated. Therefore, "if any man be in Christ"— that is, if any man is a regenerated believer in Jesus Christ as Savior— "he is a new creature," or a *changed man*. "Old things"—that is, former desires, sinful thoughts and deeds, a worldly life-style—"are passed away; behold, all things are become new." Not some things, not just one's attitude, but one's entire being becomes new. This principle of the *changed man* is at the core of Christianity. This change is not some mystical turn in the destiny of the soul only. It is a change of a way of life, sometimes of personality, appearance, outlook, values, or motivation. It is change wherever God needs to make it. It is man in sin becoming man like Christ. It is sinful man accepting Christ's finished work on the cross and then giving himself in totality to Christ for Christ to use in His way. To endeavor to minister through music without having experienced such a changed life is to grossly misunderstand the heart of the gospel as well as the nature of ministering through music. Lest one think this principle is based on only one verse, one should consider Matthew, Mark, and Luke's account of Christ's concerns before His transfiguration. He said, "Whosoever will come after me, let him deny himself, and take up his cross, and follow me. For. . .whosoever shall lose his life for my sake and the gospel's, the same shall save it" (Mark 8:34–35; see also Matt. 16:24–25 and Luke 9:23–24). Again the principle is the changed life. The salvation of a soul issues in a completely different way of life. Temptations exist as before, struggles exist between the old and new ways, but the believer has the power of the Holy Spirit to assist him in his new way thereby making the change possible. The book of James provides further support for this principle by discussing how changed behavior comes about.

GENERAL APPLICATION

How is this principle applied by the church musician? Part of the change is a change of approach. Christ's loving spirit takes control not only in the *what* but also in the *how* of behavior. Therefore Christians are to be loving and understanding in their endeavors, but that loving spirit should not be confused with indecision or weakness. If properly understood, the principles of Scripture are never at odds; rather they support each other. Thus judgments should be made in love, but they should be precise, accurate, and to the point. Following the course of least resistance or the one that may be popular, when in fact tough decisions should be made, reflects a spineless weakness, not a Christian love.

The following demonstrates the changed life principle as applied in a church music situation: *If any style of music—in its embodied or designative meaning*—creates feelings, ideas, emotions, values, or moods that are of, by, or for the unchanged way of life, such music is out of place in the changed life experience.* In other words, establishing or nurturing relationships that are directly related to the old way of life is hardly consistent new life behavior. Some music more precisely reflects the old unchanged way. Secular writers as well as Christian writers tend to agree that some of the current pop styles, for example, are lusty in their content and appeal to that part of man that is the sinful nature. The performers themselves bear witness to that fact both verbally and in the way in which they conduct themselves while performing. (It is always interesting to read reviews of secular critics who make that point in some way in their critiques. Even they are aware of the meanings of some of the current styles and they only have their musical expertise—not the added advantage of spiritual discernment—to rely on.) By contrast it seems incongruous that some Christians can disregard and openly refute such judgments. The notion that there are neither *right* nor *wrong* styles of music used by the church today seems indefensible in light of the obvious stylistic meanings and the contradiction to the changed life premises of Scripture.

My suspicions are that in time what is wrong will be proved wrong by sound musical and theological reasoning. Where questionable practices have existed, they will be found out. Christians must be honest with God and themselves. There is no virtue—biblical or otherwise—in tolerance when basic biblical principle is offended.† It would seem that some church musicians vacillate or have a double standard because of the dilemma of wanting to be in the center of the gospel pop

---

*See chapter 3 for a discussion of meaning in music.
†"Resisting the Tide," *Eternity Magazine*, July 1971, pp. 7–8.

movement and yet, on the other hand, sensing that what they do is not always consistent with what their conscience or scholarship would dictate. Very often the commercial market in the field of church music has dictated directions on the basis of what earns money for artists and music producing companies rather than on the basis of sound philosophical and theological reasoning.*

Assuming there is not total agreement as to those points of view, does the believer have any reason to run the risk of living by double standards? In the realm of church music how could it be possible that the gospel, which supposedly changes man radically, could be couched in a music language that most effectively reflects the unchanged life? Is it not more defensible as well as logical to embrace the posture that a music style that militates against the changed life in Christ is both inconsistent theologically and philosophically? If the Word of God is the authoritative guide that provides direction for all aspects of Christians' lives, then it is apparent that judgments must be made that reflect that conviction. Church music is but one area where the changed life principle is often overlooked in the total ministry of the church.

There is a trend in some theological circles today to emphasize what is sometimes referred to as a "wholistic theology." The primary thrust of that point of view suggests that there really is no sacred-secular (or sacred-profane) dichotomy to the believer. All of life is sacred, and any attempt at compartmentalization is defeating to the Christ-is-Lord-of-all perspective. When discussing that view recently with a theologian friend (who believes it to be the single most important current theological trend), it struck me that several days earlier he had mentioned he had picked up a "fuzz-buster" for his car. His all-of-life-is-sacred premise seemed to pale in my thinking as I pondered his desire to accommodate his breaking of the law through speeding. I thought, too, of my own flaws and those in the lives of friends and colleagues in the ministry and was forced to conclude that if all of life is sacred, some sacred things done by sacred individuals are certainly sinful. Backbiting, gossip, anger, obesity, and other abuses of the body, as well as countless examples of saints entrapped in culturally acceptable but biblically sinful episodes, suggest that there is or may be a credibility gap between the idealism of "all is sacred" and the realities of life.

From the perspective of *oughtness*, the believer *desires* to live all of life as a living sacrifice unto God. However, if sin is not sacred and absolute holiness is unattainable, there are moments in life that are

*Richard Dinwiddie, "Money Changers in the Church," *Christianity Today*, 26 June 1981, p. 6.

not sacred. Thank God we can still confess those moments of disobedience and be forgiven. We must desire and endeavor to live as though all of life is sacred but admit and confess those moments that are profane.

DEVELOPING A CHRISTIAN VALUE SYSTEM

This chapter has gone from a general discussion of values and God's value system to a specific example of how one can start to develop a value system. It is now time to generalize again and outline the basic requirements necessary for you, the reader, to develop your own biblical church music value system. It is apparent that one should be well equipped in the understanding and application of basic scriptural truths and musical principles. As a minimum, that implies an awareness of:

- the basic thrusts of the Old and New Testaments
- scriptural principles of godly living
- the doctrines of God, the person and work of Jesus Christ, the work of the Holy Spirit, and the Christian church's mission in the world
- the theological views of man, sin, and salvation
- all musical styles, both traditional and pop
- how music styles assume meaning

The challenge to the church musician, then, is to be not only a practitioner in the art of music but a practitioner in theology, in the psychology of music, and in philosophy. He must know how to integrate and synthesize his biblical and musical understandings into a whole perspective that results in stability, unity, and purposeful direction.

3

A Philosophy of Church Music

THE WHY—WHAT—HOW RELATIONSHIPS

When dealing with a philosophy, one must deal with the question of purpose. Concerns not only focus on the question of *how* to achieve certain ends but *why* and for *what* reasons. The logical sequence is to first determine goals or objectives (reasons for action, or the *why*), the action needed for achieving those goals (the *what*), and the methods employed in the action (the *how*). In other words, a why-what-how sequence is established to achieve continuity, unity, and cohesiveness in endeavors. There must be an internal consistency or unity among the components of the why-what-how relationship. If there is an inconsistency in type or nature between a means (how) and an end (what), or if the means leads to an end that is not what was originally desired in the objective, then philosophic integrity is nonexistent. Particularly in an "ends justify the means" philosophy that consistency must be apparent.

Church music appears to suffer presently from well-meaning musicians who recognize important or defensible goals but utilize a means of achieving those goals (ends) that is inconsistent in nature or type with the goal itself. One obvious example is when the goal is spiritual ministry, but the means leads to entertainment with little spiritual content. Another simplistic (and hopefully fallacious) example of that inconsistent approach is the story about the individual who heard the sermon on stewardship and was so moved to respond that he raised his church pledge considerably—a noble end in itself. However, in order to achieve his weekly commitment he robbed a local bank each Friday (means to the end). Although everyone easily sees the incongruity and internal inconsistency in that example, virtually the same situations occur with frequency within the church music program.

Within the framework of evangelism, for example, an "anything goes" approach is often used as long as it "brings out people." As mentioned earlier, integrity is often compromised for such a valid goal as "keeping the young people coming to church."

Certainly it is possible to attract crowds to events if there are few limitations as to the *how* of doing so. Not long ago a large church in Washington advertised that a nude female dancer would dance a "worship segment" in one of its morning services. A news magazine in reporting the occasion indicated that they packed the house. One could imagine a pastor relatively unconcerned with the inconsistency of the means of getting out the crowd as long as they got there. All too often the same level of reasoning seems to be used by well-meaning church musicians and pastors who use entertaining music forms or styles to "pack them in" but pay little attention to the paradox they create. Few pastors view their own roles as that of entertainer, yet they relegate the music program to that precise role. Undoubtedly the mass media and televised church services have influenced this trend. When entertainment ranks high on the list of objectives of the electronic church so as to capture its audience, local churches blindly follow suit.

For some musicians, in order to accommodate their own entertainment-oriented egos, the word *ministry* is substituted for the word *entertainment*. But the approach and content betray them. At best, the situation reflects inadequate understanding of philosophic consistency in means and ends; and at worst, it reflects shallow commitment and insincerity in the ministry of the Word.

MUSIC AND FUNCTION

During the Greek civilization the arts functioned as a means to an end. Music was used in conjunction with drama to support the dramatic intent of the play. Modes or systems of sound were used in conjunction with and for the purpose of evoking specific kinds of extramusical responses. One mode was used to evoke a sense of esprit de corps for the warriors of the state as they went to battle. Another was used in worship and in the expression of love for the gods. Another expressed love for fellow human beings; and they had other kinds for other occasions. People tended to respond to music depending on the mode used in somewhat predictable and specific ways. The Greeks attributed that aspect of their behavior to a supernatural or mystical power resident in the music itself. They were sure music could in fact influence for good or evil; thus, music had moral implications.

UTILITARIAN ENDS

Today it is recognized that music can evoke specific and predictable responses as well. From the time of the Greeks to the present day, music has been used in utilitarian roles to function as *means to extra-musical ends*. Rather than modes or systems of sound, as with the Greeks, people today are influenced by styles of music, or simply "the sound." There is music to shop to, dance to, march to, have teeth drilled to, love to, and, yes, worship to. Explanations as to why people tend to respond as they do to stylistic stimuli is somewhat different from the mystical supernatural notion of the Greeks. It is recognized today that people are conditioned to respond to styles through their experiences. It is true that some basic responses are intuitive, however the majority of responses are learned. People learn that a march style encourages one kind of bodily response; people also learn through conditioning that certain other styles encourage certain dances. Although they may not be total behaviorists psychologically, few musicians reject the idea that many responses to musical stimuli are the result of learned behavior. For example, a given style may evoke predictable responses in the Western civilization or within a given ethnic context but not necessarily the same response in a different culture. The Greeks accounted for predictable responses by ascribing supernatural power to the sounds. Although there are musicians today who believe that music has an intrinsic mystical power to influence for good or evil, most aestheticians support the conditioned response explanation. Regardless of what explanation of observed conditions one chooses to accept, the point to be made is that music *does* influence people to respond in predictable ways. That fact must not only be accepted by church musicians but understood and utilized to the fullest in the church music ministry.

Music, the purpose of which is to evoke extra-musical responses (shop, march, dance, worship, praise, meditate), is known to function within a utilitarian frame of reference and philosophically falls within an ends justifies the means context.

AESTHETIC ENDS

Art that exists for art's sake is art that has ends that are primarily aesthetic in nature. Historically, most vocal music created prior to the fifteenth century was of the utilitarian nature. Its purpose centered either in the experiences of the church or in social concerns (folk-singing meistersingers, minnesingers, trouveurs, and troubadours). However, as instrumental music and the instruments themselves were developed, the performance of music for sheer pleasure increased. Parlor music led to concert hall music, the purpose of which was primarily enjoyment. To this day a large percentage of music produced falls within the "aesthetic ends" category.

It is apparent that whenever one "pigeon-holes" a realm as sophisticated as an art form like music, problems of oversimplification can result. Undoubtedly there can be aspects of both utilitarian ends and aesthetic ends within given music selections. And too, what at one time in history functioned primarily within a utilitarian context (a Bach cantata, for example) may today function primarily within an aesthetic ends context. In other words, it is not only possible but probable that because of societal change in varying aspects of life, responses to age-old stimuli will change as well. Normally such changes in response are valid outgrowths of change, and performing musicians (or those who select literature for given situations) simply do so with a reasonable understanding of expected current responses. For example, no informed musician would select a waltz (triple meter) to be played while endeavoring to march. Most people have two feet with which to march and therefore are best accommodated by a selection in duple meter!

Although societal change occurs rapidly today, behavioral responses in the arts are not always able to comfortably keep pace. Within the commercial or popular realm of music, what was dance music twenty years ago is still dance music today. Love ballad styles of the forties and fifties are not dissimilar from the love ballad styles of the eighties. And yet there are church music producers, particularly in the gospel-pop area, who argue that pop styles do not produce the same responses as they did twenty years ago. They suggest that it is not at all incongruous to assume that secular love ballad styles that encourage seductive or sensual responses can, by changing the text, encourage spiritual responses. Such arguments are common among those who financially have the most to gain from the consumer of church music. Of course, today's cultural milieu is a perfect climate for such propaganda. In a day when an "if it feels good it's got to be right" philosophy of life is common, the anything goes approach to church music is right at home. Uninformed and sometimes well-meaning parishioners do not understand that what may be acceptable within one context is out of place within another.

I recall how as a young man I enjoyed jazz and popular music. (I still enjoy jazz and some pop forms.) At that time evangelicals viewed the listening to or involvement in jazz and pop music as sinful. Movies, make-up, card playing, and other vices constituted a list of "don'ts" for the serious Christian. But at the same time, within the church gospel song-writers were producing Broadway-style love ballads with "Christian" lyrics, and my colleagues in the church thought that was great! One no longer sinned if one simply changed the text within the same old musical context. I recall how my friends and I insincerely (as well as sacrilegiously) "wailed" on gospel tunes for the kicks we got out of it. Of course everyone called it "ministry" because that was the password for acceptance by the church fathers. We knew beyond question that the gut-level purpose of what we did (as well as the true responses of the listeners) was no different from that of our counterparts in the secular jazz or pop world. Today similarly immature (or commercially knowledgeable) church musicians have steered church music in that same direction.

Recently I have purposefully involved myself in situations where I could get behind the closed doors of some of the current church music pop stars and music producers. On one occasion I was to address a church music convention. I sat for two hours listening to the planning committee of supposedly mature adults debate the merits of calling a choreography workshop just that. The contention was that by calling it *staging* or *worship movement* it would get by the "old fogies" who thought dance was sinful but were "too stupid" to recognize dance as such with another name tag. Here was a group of church music leaders who prayed like all other believers I know (or at least used the same buzz words), mapping out a strategy of flagrant dishonesty and devious manipulation. That kind of Machiavellian leadership is not uncommon in some church circles today. Congregations bent on self-indulgence and pleasure are ripe prey for panderers of inappropriate music forms. If Christians recognized and accepted pop music for what it is—namely fun music primarily for entertainment—many problems would resolve themselves. It is not a question of right or wrong but one of appropriateness.

It is here that the all-of-life-is-sacred proponents might argue that if a music form is appropriate in one area of life it is appropriate in another. In other words, if pop music is acceptable or right for pleasure or clean entertainment it is also right for worship. The same logic (or lack thereof) is present in the idea that if chocolate cream pie is good for dessert it is also appropriate as the main course; or if tackling an individual is a good thing on a football field, then tackling individuals at State and Madison streets in Chicago is also a good thing. Obviously, what may be good or appropriate within one context may be totally inappropriate within another. If entertainment is a prime goal of church services then music that primarily entertains is appropriate. However, one is hard pressed to develop a biblically based argument that advocates entertainment as a primary (or even secondary) goal in church services.

THE AESTHETIC NATURE OF MAN

Much of the apparent confusion in church music today is due to a lack of understanding of the difference between music styles and their primary functions. Concert music rightfully exists for the sheer pleasure of being listened to and being performed. It is not wrong for the Christian to nurture that aspect of himself. Man, created in the image of God, was uniquely created with the propensity for the appreciation of visual and aural beauty. The great Creator gave the intellectual and emotional potential for involvement in experiences that are beautiful, rewarding, and enjoyable. In years past some preachers suggested "if you like it it must be sinful." That is not so, however. Man functions, in a sense, in the image of God when man is involved in the creative experiences of the arts. It would be naive to today suggest that a God who created man with the ability to appreciate His incredible creative acts (including a sunset or beautiful lake scene) is not pleased to have man function creatively in producing and appreciating aesthetic experiences. Great paintings, symphonies, or plays reflect some of the highest and most noble creative endeavors of man and are available for all to enjoy.

Although one does not have to be a Christian to use that God-given potential, it is only right that Christians, of all people, develop their abilities and sensitivities to the fullest and, in so doing, honor their Creator. It seems apparent that the Christian should not only conscientiously develop a few aspects of mind, body, and spirit, but strive to reach the highest potential possible for the glory of God. It is not necessary to appreciate a great choral work in order to experience the miracle of saving faith in one's life, but there is a sense in which the serious believer will utilize every opportunity to, among other things, fully develop himself aesthetically. It is therefore not inconsistent for Christians to attend concerts or for Christian performers to concertize. In the above context it is uniquely Christian.

The problem for the church musician and layperson is *to discern when a concert is a concert and when a worship service is a worship service.*

Too many worship services suffer from the malady of concert artists' performing for their audience (congregation) rather than musicians leading the congregation in a spiritual experience through the medium of music. The role of the church musician within the service (utilitarian ends) is not to use music for the primary purpose of aesthetic gratification (aesthetic ends) but to use music as a means to lead the congregation in extra-musical experiences (worship, praise, meditation, prayer, stewardship, consecration, and evangelism). The church building is not primarily a concert hall but a house of worship. Other activities legitimately transpire—including concerts—in the church, but the primary purpose of the assembled Body of Christ is to worship its God. The performer's ego must be held in check to enable the decision-making process to consistently support the spiritual goals of the service.

That does not preclude all aesthetic considerations. As a matter of fact, a spiritually wise and mature church musician does not select cheap or trite music but the best available that also convincingly achieves the intended spiritual experience. His best creative efforts are not used to achieve salvation or to be better accepted by God—the best that can be offered to God is never enough to attain salvation. Rather, he gives God his creative best out of a heart of love and out of gratitude for the free gift of salvation. It is not only musically weak but spiritually immature to offer God less than one's best in any act of service, in any realm whatsoever. There may be a place for trite experiences for the Christian, but certainly in the realm of the spirit one does well not to compromise.

In summary, all music falls within two broad categories: utilitarian ends and aesthetic ends. The Christian should be knowledgeably involved in both areas, using discernment as to appropriateness and utilization of either. The variables that determine how music functions are the cultural patterns of the given time and place taken together with the more intrinsic aspects of the music itself. It would seem logical that one could determine how a style would best function on the basis of its *primary intent*. Although a piece might be capable of evoking extra-musical responses as well as aesthetic responses, one can determine where it best functions on the basis of its primary intent. Therefore, a given piece may primarily cause people to respond by marching or dancing, but a secondary by-product may be sensual or aesthetic gratification. To apply that principle to church music, aesthetic gratification may be a legitimate response, but it should be strictly secondary. The primary response should be worship or praise. If that is not the order in which responses occur, the music is no longer service music but concert music that functions under aesthetic ends.

STYLE IN MUSIC

STYLE DEFINED

It becomes apparent that music that can be categorized must have distinguishing characteristics that, when heard by the listener, may be recognized. The characteristics thus identifiable are referred to as *style, idiom,* or, currently, *the sound.* Style in music is what the musician studies in an endeavor to produce accuracy in performance. The identifiable characteristics that make a Beethoven symphony sound different from a Brahms symphony, or acid rock different from folk rock, is *style.* Style is the way in which the elements (melody, harmony, and rhythm) of music are combined. Musicians deal with two areas of style: the *composer's style* (Bach's approach in the Baroque style) and the *performance style* (as exemplified by Sir Thomas Beecham's performance of the *Messiah* versus Robert Shaw's). Musicians endeavor to faithfully recreate the music according to their stylistic understanding. Why is it that some give their entire lives to the study of style? Why is it that almost every music appreciation textbook written deals with style in music? The obvious answer is that *it is through style that music assumes much of its meaning to the listener.* Certainly in vocal music concrete meaning is arrived at through texts. But as far as the music is concerned, meaning, both concrete and abstract, designative and embodied,* is generally arrived at through style. In other words, as people are aware of style and its implications through conditioning and psychological associations along with their intuitions, music assumes meaning. Therefore music is probably not a universal language as some have romantically suggested. It is a language that becomes intelligible as any other spoken language becomes intelligible. Each style (Renaissance, Baroque, Classic, Romantic, Modern, 1930 dixie, 1940 boogie-woogie, 1969 rock, or 1980 disco) has its own set of meanings. To know how to use or to understand music becomes the task of understanding style. Leonard B. Meyer states that "style constitutes the universe of discourse within which musical meanings arise."† Style is to music as language is to verbal communication; communication takes place when the listener is conversant with the style.

VERBAL COMMUNICATION

When communicating verbally, words assume meaning as a language (including a vocabulary) is understood. In order to communi-

---

*See pages 25–27 for explanations of *designative* and *embodied.*
†Leonard B. Meyer, *Music, the Arts and Ideas,* p. 7.

cate verbally one must speak English, German, or whatever the language is in which one intends to communicate. Although concrete levels of meaning can come close to being arrived at through verbal communication, there can be a gap between the one who communicates and the one to whom the communication is directed. Excluding the obvious difficulties of the communication process, it is readily apparent that there is little chance of communication's taking place unless a common language is spoken.

NON-VERBAL COMMUNICATION

Non-verbal communication is when communication takes place without the use of words. In arriving at meaning in the communication process, one is clearly affected by the body language that is used by the communicator. As a matter of fact, the body language may betray the true intention of the communicator. One can normally use body language as a clue of support or nonsupport of what is in fact said. Importance of meaning can be underlined by the manner in which something is stated. Good communicators develop every aspect of non-verbal communication to assist in effective communication. The theater capitalizes on non-verbal communication to assist in the powerful communication intent.

In the realm of music, non-verbal communication is created by the musical style, for it is through the sounds of music—the style—that music assumes meaning. Style in music can be equated with nonverbal communication, or body language. Just as gestures, facial expressions, tone of voice, and inflections give rise to meaning so also do the sounds of music apart from any attached text. In church music where so much of what is performed has texts, listeners are often only tuned in to meanings that arise from the text. However, the whole set of meanings that arise solely from the sounds are often not subtle, being obvious to the listener who knows the language. If one is going to arrive at meaning through any given style of music, one must know the style. (The same is true in verbal communication.) If listeners are unaware of the meaning of a given selection of music (assuming they understand the language of the text), the apparent reason is that they do not understand the style of the music itself.

It is precisely for that reason that those who advocate the utilization of pop styles in church music suggest that such styles are most appropriate inasmuch as they are the styles that are best understood by the masses. The so-called classical styles are understood by a much smaller group of individuals and therefore would be inappropriate for utilization in the average church service. If the debate were to stop at that point, I would be pressed to agree. However, when it becomes a matter of appropriateness of style penetrating beyond the surface of mere acquaintance to implications of meanings, more serious complications force this writer to disagree. The meanings, feelings, and moods of pop music are well known. The meanings are beautifully united in the "secular" forms, and the pop world uses them appropriately. The question is, Does the meaning change by changing the text? The concern here is not to point out the inadequacy or inappropriateness of some pop music styles for utilization in the church and thereby imply that only Brahms, Beethoven, or Bach are appropriate. Rather, it is the church musician's responsibility to locate those styles that are consistent in their meanings with the meanings and intentions of the objectives of the service. Surface level meanings that are appropriate as entertainment and fun are normally not what most churches desire as their spiritual food. Such trivia knowingly desired would be an indictment of the theology and purpose of the church.

If in fact music assumes meaning to people through style, it becomes obvious that in order to determine whether or not a style of music should be used, one must first of all analyze the style to determine what types of responses may be expected. Some appropriate and revealing questions are:

- What meaning does this music have to those who use it within the culture?
- Out of what kinds of values does it come?
- What kinds of people use it and *how* do they use it?
- What does it mean to those who most frequently use it?

One must also determine whether or not the expected responses are the desired responses or determine if the meaning in the music is what is desired. In other words, are the meanings of the music consistent with the purposes or ends of the service? Needing to recondition a subculture so as to provide new meanings to accommodate a given style is sufficient to cause the integrity of such attempts to be questioned. Moreover, it simply does not work. The meanings of styles in the broad world culture simply cannot be replaced by small church subcultures regardless of the amount of well-intentioned effort. Pop music styles by virtue of their roots and content reflect the pop world culture and the accompanying meanings. Simply changing the words will not change the meanings of the sounds.

A sensitivity to appropriateness of music style is developed through an awareness of both style itself and the context of that style in the world. Church musicians must therefore be conversant with all music styles and be culturally aware. It is not necessary to become a part of the world to achieve that. They simply must open their eyes and ears in order to see and hear how various music idioms are used. It quickly becomes apparent that what some music styles mean is diametrically opposed to the verbal communication of spiritual texts.

The church musician has the additional task of insuring that his musical values be consistent with and supportive of his theological views. Care must be taken that cultural patterns and meanings of the unregenerated world do not infiltrate the church, causing the church to no longer speak with authority in matters of the spirit. When the music of the church functions as a vehicle for fun and entertainment rather than as a focal point for worship, praise, and other spiritual experiences, clearly the life blood of the church is being sapped.

MEANING IN MUSIC

DESIGNATIVE MEANING

Designative meaning is "when a stimulus or process indicates or refers to something which is different from itself in kind—as when a word denotes an object or concept which is not itself a word."* An example is when the word *chair* refers to an object upon which people sit. In other words, the word *chair* designates such an object. Within the realm of music, writers refer to that kind of meaning as extramusical meaning. Designative meaning in music is when a tympani roll represents thunder, a flute or piccolo part represents birds chirping, or specific orchestral colors create moods or feelings that are outside of the music itself. Football fans may recall having chills go down their spines upon hearing their old alma mater rouser played. That sense of esprit de corps is a learned kind of meaning. The rouser (often in a march style) refers back to meanings that are outside of the music itself. Such meaning results from both an awareness of the musical style within a cultural context and a conditioning to the stimulus itself. Whenever music is used to evoke extra-musical responses (i.e., emotions, bodily responses, or spiritual responses), it is based upon the concept of designative meaning and is functioning within a utilitarian context.

Designative meanings are therefore those meanings that arise out of a musical style (the stimulus) and evoke highly predictable responses that are primarily extra-musical or extra-aesthetic. The world of music therapy as well as the radio and television commercials of Madison Avenue have researched ways in which human behavior can be manipulated through designative meaning. Increased spending in

*Meyer, p. 6.

stores where happy music is played through the sound system, a quieting of the nerves in the dentist chair, the purchase of a given product because of a remembered "happy" commercial, or thoughts of passion are all examples of ways in which people respond to designative meanings through styles.

EMBODIED MEANING

Embodied meaning is when "a stimulus or process acquires meanings because it indicates or refers to something which is like itself in kind."* Within the realm of verbal communication, embodied meaning is when *word* denotes a word. Embodied meaning is intrinsic to the stimulus or process, and the meaning that arises will be within the context of that stimulus or process. In the realm of music this form of meaning is referred to as *musical meaning*. Within the context of a given style, "one tone or group of tones that leads the practiced listener to expect another tone or group of tones to be forthcoming" assumes embodied meaning.†

This kind of meaning is less precise and necessarily more abstract than designative meaning and yet is satisfying and worthy of pursuit. One has to know a given style with some certainty in order to arrive at embodied meaning. Musicians and many music lovers move beyond the level of designative meaning into embodied meaning because they find it so fulfilling. It is the differentiation between the two levels of meaning that delineates the representational content in music (designative meaning) and the nonrepresentational music content (embodied meaning). Rimsky-Korsakov's *Scheherezade* or Richard Strauss's *Death and Transfiguration* are examples of representational works replete with designative meanings. The fourth symphony of Brahms probably carries little if any designative meaning potential but is a profound experience in embodied meaning for those who are attuned to Brahms's style.

To the musician, textual communication is only part of the whole realm of communication. The educated musician will be as much or perhaps more aware of the levels of communication that take place through the sounds themselves. Those sounds are the realm of musical meanings that so few in the ministry and in church music understand. It is not abnormal for a pastor to be incapable of analyzing the style of a given piece to know the implied meanings, therefore

*Ibid.
†Ibid., pp. 6–7.

most analyses done are textual ones rather than musical ones. But to analyze text alone is to do only 50 percent of the job; the other 50 percent is to analyze the music styles. It is the responsibility of church musicians to be informed and lead the way in arriving at the meanings of any given style. That is not to say that the text is unimportant or should not be carefully considered.

In endeavoring to determine the appropriateness of a piece of music, the problem then is not only a textual one but a musical one. It is common knowledge among choral musicians that if the music does not appropriately support the implications and meanings of a text, the piece is not a good piece and is unworthy of performance. (It is said that there is a bad wedding between the text and music.) When there are literally thousands of pieces where the music fits the text and the text fits the music, it is highly questionable for any individual to choose selections where a paradox of meanings can be created. Yet some current trends are best characterized by just such a paradox.

SUMMARY AND APPLICATION

In summary, music assumes meaning, both designative and embodied, as performers and listeners understand the style. Music—that is pitches, harmonies, melodic lines, and rhythms—does not intrinsically mean. People give meaning to the sounds through their conditioned and intuitive responses. The capacity for a satisfying level of understanding is directly related to the individual's stylistic awareness. The church musician cannot assume that ignorance is bliss. Although many people cannot give specific reasons as to why they think there can be duality of meaning between styles and texts, they at least will have some intuitive awareness that a paradox is created. Regardless, it is the musician's responsibility to lead the way and not capitalize on and take advantage of a lack of musical awareness in the congregation. To perpetuate trends that rely on naiveté in the church is hypocritical at best. Trite words should give rise to trite music. Profound words and ideas should give rise to profound music. There are many hymns that are very simply written but are profound in both their musical and textual content.

The musician must always analyze the text and the music separately. A musician must not allow a text to subjectively predetermine the meanings of a piece. It is important to analyze the *sounds of the music* completely separated from any given text. Separate analysis is necessary to ascertain that there is congruity in the feelings, moods, and meanings of both the text and the music style. If there is incongruity, the piece should be judged to be unworthy of use.

Some time ago I recall hearing a piece based on the text "When I Survey the Wondrous Cross." It was set to an upbeat flippant style that rendered the piece a paradox of paradoxes. The cross and its implications are only worthy of a musical support that has profundity, sobriety, and an awareness of what Christ's death cost. To sing of the wondrous cross in a flippant manner reflects not only a stylistic lack of awareness but a spiritual unawareness as well. A similar incongruity is reflected in a number of gospel songs of recent years dealing with the theme of the joy of the Christian. Once again, the incongruity of the joy motif as reflected in the style of the music is readily apparent. On the one hand, theologically it is said that the joy of the Lord surpasses anything the world can offer and is of a spiritual nature. Yet the music style often reflects the fun of the life of sin. The dilemma probably resulted from either the song writers' being musically inadequate to express the joy of the Lord or from their not being spiritually sensitized to the differences that exist between the joy of the world and the joy of the Lord.

One other trend that needs to be questioned is the use of seductive love ballad styles that focus on Jesus Christ as the erotic lover. The language used—both musical and textual—to describe the agape love relationship of the Lord and Savior must of necessity not smack of today's lusty, sensuous, cheap love. The true tragedy of the situation may not lie in the fact that there is a disparity between the text and musical style, but may be in the fact that the paradox is an accurate commentary on the spiritual life of the church itself. Can it be that the joy or love that is proclaimed by the church is in fact the same joy or love that the world expresses through its pleasure? Certainly some current church music trends lead to that conclusion.

TEXT AND MUSIC ANALYSIS

THE TEXT

It is only right to expect careful analysis of a text in determining suitability for any music performance situation and, most important, the church service. The choral musician and the church musician commonly develop music skills as other musicians do but also deal with the art of text or literature, consequently needing skills in textual analysis as well. Regardless of the situation, the text usually reflects at least 50 percent of the whole communication element. In church music, the text carries the more concrete verbal levels of meaning and is therefore vitally important to the achievement of spiritual communication.

In recent years there have been societal trends to downplay correctness of grammar, syntax, and beauty of speech. Educated young people (as well as their parents) often deliberately use incorrect speech so as to not appear too sophisticated or intelligent. One hears "it don't matter" and "there's lots of" with considerable frequency among educated people. Where there is a waning emphasis placed upon excellence of speech, the same trend can be expected to influence texts of songs. That is one of the areas where cultural trends have had a questionable influence on the church. The relevance concern has encouraged the inclusion of colloquialisms and trendy expressions in texts by songwriters who hope to be "with it." Unfortunately, in the same vein many marvelous and worthy hymn texts have been altered in recent hymnbook publications so as to render them current. There is no problem with change where the poetic or artistic integrity is maintained—if there was any in the first place. However, change that issues in weakness and plays to trends that tend to encourage less thoughtful involvement by the participants, yet goes under the disguise of encouraging increased involvement, needs to be strongly objected to. In a sense, Shakespeare is dated (there are probably those who would like to modernize his language), but it is timeless to those who are willing to exert the intellectual energy of an involvement and appreciation of great art. "I'm thinking of killing myself," although an accurate paraphrase, can never have the impact of Hamlet's "To be, or not to be, that is the question." Shakespeare has a powerful communication potential that supersedes vocabularies based upon three-letter words.

In addition to negative cultural influences, buzz word syndromes influence church music texts. It may not be long before there is a song suggesting how *super* Jesus is and how *super* one should feel as a result. The "really really" generation searches for authenticity of experience and endeavors to express that search in trite language. "I'm *really* glad that Jesus is *really* my friend, and I *really* know that He'll *really* go with me to the end." It is little wonder, then, that some church music texts focus on relevant buzz word language and superficial subjective experiences resulting in both questionable language and content. Far too many texts are "I" or "how I feel" in orientation. Scriptural truth is often referred to casually—if at all. What often finds its way into some churches as contemporary gospel music is textually quasi-religious at best, with little or no solid scriptural basis and focus.

An analysis of texts for the purpose of spiritual communication and spiritual response is therefore critical. A text must not only coincide with basic biblical premises but should reflect the integrity and value of the Word itself. When dealing with eternal values and the souls of mankind, shoddy or "cute" texts do not enhance the import of the message. Certainly subjective experiences focusing on the individual rather than the Godhead are chancy anyway. People's feelings change with great frequency. However, God does not change. The subjective response of man to God's work in the world and one's life are important. But subjective experience as a singular diet is disastrous to the nurture and growth of the believer. The gospel must be presented in simplicity and clarity, yet its integrity should not be impuned in the process. Ultimately there is no contradiction between the ideals of simplicity and correctness.

The solution in contemporary music is to encourage the development of literary and poetic skills of authors and not accept marginal materials unworthy of a musician's time and effort, much less God's glorification. Careful scrutiny as to theological consistency with the teachings of the Word as well as appropriate language will help to eliminate unworthy texts and will provide the stimulus for helpful spiritual experience. Also, a willingness to experience spiritual truth through historically proved texts should not be unthinkable. Even today, young people can learn to use and love old hymn texts if the hymns are approached positively. Thinking young people are as much concerned about froth in spiritual experience as are older generations. The current trend of using Scripture verses set to folk-style music is a positive and hopeful example of that concern.

THE MUSIC

Music analysis is often more difficult for some church musicians than is textual analysis. In order to ascertain appropriateness of musical style one has to be conversant with all of the styles currently extant, with the way those styles are primarily used, and with the normal contexts of their meanings. Within the realm of the classics, a stylistic awareness of Gregorian, Renaissance, Baroque, Classic, Romantic, and a number of twentieth-century styles is needed. In addition, if one adds to the list all of the pop, jazz, rock, folk, and gospel styles, the task may seem formidable. But of all the members of the church staff, if the church musicians do not know style and lead the congregation in meaningful music experiences, who will? All too often, musicians build cases of appropriateness or inappropriateness based on textual analysis alone. People do not need to be musicians to analyze texts. A church musician needs the skills not only to perform various styles accurately but to understand them as well. To be a fine conductor, organist, or singer is not enough. Performance skills are important, but they do not prepare musicians for the necessary decision-making process. Having a great talent as an orchestrator, arranger, or organist does not qualify an individual to lead the church in understanding the theological, philosophical, or psychological aspects of the music used. As mentioned earlier, practitioners of the art are strictly that and no more.

THE INFLUENCES OF "NEW" CHRISTIANS

It is no more reasonable for church music directions to be determined by name musicians who are new believers than it is for the theology of the church to be determined by a newly converted philosophy major. Being able to effectively, logically reason in the Socratic method does not qualify one in theology. Because one can play the piano or create beautiful orchestrations does not mean that one is philosophically qualified in church music. The analysis of the music score in church music is a process involving

- the awareness and integration of music styles, theology, and Scripture
- the applying of that analysis to church service objectives
- the anticipation of (and capitalizing on) how people respond to and normally use the styles in question

That synthesis and integration of knowledge can only take place by one who is not only mature in the skills of music but also mature in the skills of understanding Scripture. Nowhere in Scripture is there the suggestion that if one becomes a believer the regeneration experience will also provide a supernatural wisdom on matters of church music. A style that, for example, encourages a burlesque queen to remove her clothes is not going to have a different meaning because some religious words have been added and it is performed in a Sunday evening church service rather than a theater. The commercial pop styles selling sex or toothpaste only cheapen the gospel message when a religious text replaces the old one. Pandering Jesus Christ in the same idiom as a television commercial does a gross injustice to the ministry and message of Christ. Yet the church has sometimes been led to believe that such allegations are false and only a figment of the imagination of overly educated stodgy church musicians. Time after time serious scholars of church music who do know better have been unjustly minimized by new Christians or others who somehow refuse basic logic.

I will not soon forget a conversation I overheard a few years ago by several "outsiders" from a secular university when the song "He Touched Me" was being crooned. At first the young people began giggling at the text sung by the sultry female. They quieted down after a while, but their response to the text, the music style, and the performance style (which included every sensual gimmick a seductive female singer could use) was appropriate. Not long after that experience I heard the same opening phrase sung by a woman on a television commercial advertising Chantilly perfume. The gist of the message of the commercial was "he touched me" (in the physical sense) because she had the perfume on. The sensual style was appropriate for the occasion, and there was total congruity between the seductive performance style, the text, and the music. If people responded honestly to the music styles of much of what they hear in church services today, the church would become just another theater or nightclub setting with the expected responses of such establishments. There is nothing wrong with clean entertainment per se. However, I believe the church has a different mission in the world.

By now, there are undoubtedly readers who have questions concerning how certain styles, if they are so inappropriate, can be the source of so much blessing. How can it be that such styles can apparently lead so many to the Lord? One possible answer may lie in how one defines *blessing*. The word is often used as a buzz word within a context more suitable to the words *fun, joy, pleasure*, or *aesthetic gratification*. Young people in my college choir often have difficulty discerning the difference between a blessing and an aesthetic experience. They prefer to use the word *blessing* because it sounds more spiritual, or it may be that they have honestly misinterpreted what is actually aesthetic in nature as being spiritual. If an experience results in spiritual insight or it is primarily in the realm of scriptural or spiritual truth, the word *blessing* is then appropriate. If it is another way of saying, "I enjoyed the music," then that is something else. What some people think is a blessing is more likely a pleasurable experience with little true spiritual fiber.

Secular aestheticians do not differentiate between the spiritual and aesthetic realms. To them, all such experience is spiritual. For that reason many people find their spiritual food at symphony concerts or other art experiences. It is therefore necessary for the believer to differentiate between those two realms, or the logical result leads to a diminishing of the need for Holy Spirit led (spiritual) experience.

As to the question of so many being saved, it would be difficult to prove that it was the music style that saved them. Undoubtedly pop styles can gain the attention of the young people—and others as well. But most likely it is the truth of the Word textually that specifically reaches the hearts. Scripture states that God's Word will not return to Him void (Isa. 55:11). The sowing of the Word through music of varying styles is possible. To the casual listener why should the church not use serious scriptual texts with music that is fun and alive with emotion? The answer is that *the Word deserves more than secular, fun level experience.* God the Spirit often works in spite of man's feeble efforts to accomplish His will. In evangelism it is not so much that a style results in converts as it is that the Spirit of God works through a text. Undoubtedly, the same people could have become Christians with the same text set to an excerpt of a symphony or "Yankee Doodle." It is important that church musicians not mislead themselves into thinking that it was a specific style that did the work any more than it is the *body language* of the pastor in preaching his sermon that causes people to come to Christ. It is the work of the Holy Spirit that issues in changed life experiences, not the pastor's delivery or the musical style. However, that does not remove from musicians the responsibility of giving Him their best and utilizing their skills to convey spiritual truth. Thinking people seeking spiritual truth deserve the most consistent product and best method of hearing that truth. The question, then, is not, What can we get by with and still lead people into a spiritual experience? Rather, it is, How can the Word best be presented through consistent meanings between texts and music styles? A proper answer will lead to the use of the art of music with no tinge of profanation.

Needless to say, what is here advocated will not be popular with record companies, music publishers, and the Christian pop musicians who base their business on music trends.* However, it is time for the church to formulate its philosophy of church music on the basis of thoughtfully informed insight rather than blindly buying every new money-making scheme introduced by the pop music industry. Church musicians and pastors must provide leadership in resisting the tide of inappropriate literature flooding the scene.

SOME ANSWERS

If one, in good conscience, is to reject much of what is today produced as church music, what are the alternatives? Problems are often easily ascertained, but valid solutions are sometimes evasive. In any evaluative procedure it is important to—as objectively as possible—see whatever good exists in areas thought to be broadly harmful. The following are suggestions as to how to avoid using inappropriate music yet maintain the interest of the entire congregation, young and old.

Education. Use every available opportunity to tactfully educate the congregation in the use of music in the church. Articles in church

*Richard Dinwiddie, "Moneychangers in the Church," *Christianity Today*, 26 June 1981, p. 16.

papers or bulletins, church music classes for worship committees and others of the congregation, and explanations of textual and musical meanings to all performers in rehearsals are an ongoing and vital part of every church musician's ministry. Questions by anyone such as, "Why can't we sing songs like 'I Wanna Rock with the Rock of Ages'?" are indicators of what needs to be done educationally in the church. Comments or questions concerning any aspect of the church music program are usually serious and reflect an honest concern. An effective church musician capitalizes on such opportunities and develops a multifaceted educational program touching all departments of the church.

Involvement. The most effective education takes place when the church regularly experiences appropriate music through meaningful involvement. *Good* or *great** music performed poorly is the quickest avenue to requests for questionable literature. Musicians who select literature too difficult for their choir's performance and congregation's meaningful involvement are inviting trouble. It is far better to use simple yet good literature within the range of available performance skills than to use difficult literature far beyond everyone's reach. Effective music ministry is not only a matter of "getting through" a piece; it is a question of mastering it sufficiently so as to get out of the way of the music in order that it may effectively communicate. When musicians have to focus most of their intellectual and emotional energies on the techniques of performance, they usually sacrifice the joy of being ministers of the message. I fear that many well-meaning musicians make the mistake of choosing literature reflecting their own musical capabilities rather than those with whom they work. As choirs and congregations grow in skill and insight, the level of literature used can also grow. If too large a gap develops in that regard, the church musician will lose his effectiveness in the leadership role.

Nurturing. Church musicians and pastors need to nurture the notion that it is not necessary to use music from the Top 40 on the charts of gospel music publishers to have relevant spiritual experiences. As *new* should not be blindly equated with *appropriate* by young people, so also *old* should not be blindly equated with *appropriate* by older people. There are old hymns and gospel songs no more worthy than the most trite new song. As a matter of fact, some of the most trite gospel songs of the forties and fifties were the forerunners or the generic heritage of today's trite songs. Some of the great classics musically have texts no more worthy of consideration than some of the current texts. It is

*See p. 97 for technical definitions of *good* and *great*.

essential, therefore, that the church musician have the necessary textual and musical skills to effectively evaluate literature of all styles.

One has only to multiply the number of minutes spent by the number of people involved (performers and congregation) to arrive at the total man hours wasted in superficial experience. Just as a pastor may some day be held accountable for the wasted time for which he has been responsible in the pulpit, so may the church musician be held accountable. It is a serious thing not to use precious time as effectively as possible in the world of the Spirit. Time wasted in entertaining endeavors under the disguise of spiritual experience will some day be accounted for. The selection of literature and effective involvement of all in the music experiences are matters of serious consequence and must therefore be carefully planned for and carried out.

Consistency. A total music program will suffer and crumble from within if all literature used in all departments of a church does not meet the tests of suitability. In some churches the music literature used in the morning worship service is worthy, but in the Sunday school or youth groups the literature is trite. It is as though the church says, "Our children are worthy only of ditties that create meaningless spiritual experience," or "Our young people only want to sing for the fun of it, not for profound spiritual involvement." It may be that the young people only enjoy certain styles; but if their services are supposedly for reasons other than sheer pleasure, such concern is misplaced. It is true that much youth music is best used for social purposes, but the objectives of the gatherings are also in need of evaluation. Churches often underestimate the intellectual and emotional sophistication of today's young people and continue feeding them musical Pablum rather than steak. In public schools young people can do math problems and deal with abstractions far more advanced than prior generations. The sophistication of some of their educational experiences greatly surpass their experiences at church. It is as though the church says to today's young person, "Do your thinking in school, but come to church to play games." My personal experience has been that young people will become involved in music experiences that have substance if they are so encouraged and if they experience them at a qualitative level of excellence. As with adults, youth choirs singing good literature poorly is disastrous. However, young people singing good literature with a relatively high level of excellence will do so with the greater enthusiasm they have for performing some of the poor youth music that they seem to enjoy.

In my own church our high school choir presently averages ninety-five singers who rehearse Tuesday nights for one-and-one-half hours,

Sunday mornings for one hour, sing at two worship services every Sunday, and always sing solid and meaningful selections. In addition, the choir presents "The Seven Last Words of Christ," by Dubois, every year with orchestra and soloists, as well as taking part in other concert opportunities. The young people like jazz and pop music like all young people do today, but when it comes to spiritual experiences they are taught that there is a difference. The skeptics always believe that today's kids will only take part in "Contemporary Christian" music styles. There are a number of churches in addition to my own where that assertion is regularly proved wrong.

It is only a matter of time before the church using bad literature with young people will experience the creeping paralysis of bad literature in the worship service. After all, the young people are the future members of the church. What they know by experience they bring with them through life into adulthood. Young people who only know pop music experiences in youth services and Sunday school will soon expect those same experiences in worship services. The surest path to future weakness is to begin with compromises in the youth programs of the church. Conversely, the best insurance for continued meaningful worship and praise experiences musically is to teach it and implement it in the early years. The result is harmony and unity with no credibility gap between the young and the old of the congregation. Youth music of necessity may be a bit simpler than that used by adults, but it need not be inferior.

Analysis. An analysis of both text and music is essential in ascertaining the suitability of any literature for use in services. Literature is worthy only when the textual and musical meanings coincide and are consistent with the objectives of the service. The avoidance of music-text paradoxes such as those listed below is essential:

Music	Text
Trite	Profound
Lighthearted	Serious
Serious	Lighthearted
Sensual	Spiritual
Happy	Sorrowful
Sorrowful	Happy

A good wedding of text and music always results in supportive reinforcement of moods, feelings, and meanings when analyzed both musically and textually. Many years ago, Fred Waring made a statement that I have never forgotten. It is clearly applicable to the point at hand: "If you can't sing it better than you can say it, why sing it?"

4

Music in Worship

A HUMAN-DIVINE ENCOUNTER

A great deal of space is given in church music books to the question of worship and ways in which music can function as a vehicle of worship. Authors such as Austin C. Lovelace and William C. Rice, Erik Routley, Carl Schalk, and Don Hustad* (to name a few) have all effectively dealt with the topic. These distinguished authors have clearly emphasized the theological focus of worship and the need of the believer to regularly worship his God. The healthy perspective that all of life should be lived as an act of worship of God is not at all at odds with the admonition to not be "forsaking the assembling of ourselves together" (Heb. 10:25). Romans 12:1–2 admonishes believers to present their bodies as holy, living sacrifices, that are acceptable to God and to do that as an act of service—or *worship*. Believers are not to conform to this world (food for thought in evaluating appropriateness of music styles for worship) but to be transformed by the renewing of their minds so that they may ultimately know God's good, pleasing,

*Austin C. Lovelace and William C. Rice, *Music and Worship in the Church*; Erik Routley, *Words, Music and the Church*; Carl Schalk, *Church Music and the Christian Faith* and *Key Words in Church Music*; Don Hustad, *Jubilate*.

and perfect will. The socialization of the act of corporate worship has in some churches resulted in a kind of uninspiring unfocused experience. Because of an emphasis on individual worship as a common daily experience, the corporate experience is downgraded to a socializing and fellowship status. To neglect one aspect of the whole renders the individual one-sided.

Scripture clearly teaches a daily walk that maintains an open communion with God, but it also clearly teaches the need for the body of believers to regularly and seriously worship God. Balance must be emphasized. Because church music is a vehicle of corporate worship it is within the music context that worship will here be considered.

WORSHIP BEGINS WITH GOD

Psalm 27:8 states: "When thou saidst, Seek ye my face; my heart said unto thee, Thy face, Lord, will I seek." Worship is man's response to the nature of God. Someone has said, "It is the acknowledgement of the 'worthship' of God."

WORSHIP IS COMMANDED BY GOD

Worship is never an act of man based upon his own merit with the intention of satisfying man's desires. It satisfies God's command first, and then the experience benefits man. One does not worship because one enjoys it or it feels good (aesthetic reasons). One worships God because He alone is worthy, and He expects it.

WORSHIP NEEDS TO BE ENCOURAGED

The elements used as vehicles (speech, music, architecture, visual symbols, apparel worn by leaders and choirs, acoustics, and instruments) must all reinforce, encourage, and function in the implementation of the worship experience. None of the vehicles exist as ends in themselves. They are means to the end (utilitarian ends) of worship. If that premise were kept in mind from the construction of the church building on through all aspects of program planning such as music selection and sermon preparation, a number of things would be done differently by the institutional church. If people were convinced of the importance of the regular corporate experience, sanctuaries would not look like roller-skating rinks, gymnasiums, or theaters; choirs would not look or sound like "The Joe Schmo Singers" of the weekly television variety show; the organ would not sound like the local bar organ complete with its whirling electronic multi-speed vibratos; and the acoustics of the church would not remind one of the local sound re-cording studio with deadening materials everywhere. It is only rea-sonable that every means possible should be used to *encourage the wor-shiper to profoundly and meaningfully respond to his Maker's call to worship.*

WORSHIP IS THE FOCAL POINT OF THE CHRISTIAN LIFE

From the point in time the individual becomes a member of the Body of Christ, he must focus on the worship of his Lord. All other aspects of his spiritual walk with the Lord radiate out from the central worship experience.

WORSHIP HAS A PATTERN

The worship experience itself has both objective and subjective ele-ments that are important to a balanced worship endeavor. The se-quence of Isaiah 6—which is generally followed by liturgical churches and some non-liturgical churches—is not one of chance but of prac-ticality. In studying the passage a definite pattern can be recognized.

- The believer enters the presence of God.
- The believer is confronted with the holiness and righteousness of God and realizes his own inadequacy. That awareness issues in conviction of sin, a sense of personal guilt and need for forgiveness, and the confession of one's sins.
- God enlightens, transforms, renews, and purifies the believer.
- God the Spirit nourishes the life of the believer through His Word, resulting in spiritual growth (education).
- The believer is challenged to live out his faith in the world. He pre-sents his life and material goods (stewardship) to God for His use. The result is the church witnessing (evangelism), sharing (social concerns), and living all aspects of life so as to glorify God.

WORSHIP IS AN OBJECTIVE EXPERIENCE

It is self-evident that the objective aspects of worship are best sup-ported by objective vehicles and music styles. Thinking of God as He is—perfect, holy, unchanging, just, all-knowing, all-present—is gen-erally best reflected in the styles of more objective hymn texts and hymn tunes and/or some liturgical settings. Entering the presence of perfection and sinlessness is best done with a sense of reverence, awe, wonder, and adoration. Straightforward, objective styles help create those experiences as long as the worshiper understands the meaning of worship itself and engages his or her mind and emotions in the process. It is at those points in the worship experience that the great hymns of the church and profound anthems have their place.

WORSHIP IS A SUBJECTIVE EXPERIENCE

It is also self-evident that the subjective aspects of worship are best supported by subjective vehicles and music styles. The relief from the burden of sin, the overwhelming sense of gratitude to the Lord for the gift of salvation (which cost Him His life yet was totally free to the worshiper), and the resulting commitment of life and talents to His service are all aspects of the subjective worship element. Hymns that reflect that subjectivity textually and stylistically are appropriate as are good gospel hymns and folksongs. Just as it is important for the worshiper to be confronted with the profundity of the objective aspects of the worship experience, so it is also important for subjective personalization (the "it was for me" awareness) to take place. Christ's claims upon "my" life and "my" response are vital to the total work of the Lord in the world to say nothing of the salvation of "my" soul. The mission of the church is only realized when the church meets God in worship regularly and then actively responds. An imbalance of one aspect over the other (objectivity versus subjectivity) or even an absence of either (as is the case in some churches) issues in lopsided lives and an imbalanced church. Intellectualism alone produces coldness and indifference, whereas emotionalism alone produces instability. Slight variations on those themes are not unhealthy but on the contrary provide experiences with which people of varying backgrounds and understandings identify. The church of Christ, thankfully, is made up of people who approach these matters in a variety of ways, and diversity within overarching unifying elements is healthy.

> Securing a proper balance between the objective and subjective aspects of worship constitutes the main problem in Protestant church worship. Our theology of God conditions our worship perspective. Some see God primarily as transcendent, others as immanent. But man's nature cries out for both a sense of the ultimate and the intimate. When men magnify one at the expense of the other, spiritual experience is in danger of becoming either cold and legalistic, or over-familiar and sentimental. The true worship of God is a blend of both awe and love. Basically it is the problem of making God real—the miracle that should happen every time man gathers for worship.*

Churches that are imbalanced in objective-subjective content, upon in-

---

*James D. Robertson, "The Nature of Christian Worship," *Asbury Seminarian* 2 (1953):28.

stituting greater balance in experience, soon discover or rediscover how meaningful worship can be.

WORSHIP SHOULD BE FOSTERED BY MUSIC

The primary purpose of all service music is to evoke or encourage the above experiences. One evaluates or determines the value of service music on its potential of succeeding with a specific group of worshipers in mind. The functioning potential of any selection is determined against the backdrop of the congregation. Music for a hill folk service will, of necessity, be different from that used in suburbia. Cultural, educational, and intellectual backgrounds must be considered as well as chronological and spiritual maturity. But it is inappropriate to accommodate any of the above through compromise. Devious means of accommodation are inconsistent with the essence of the gospel, and such intent is at serious odds with Scripture itself. It becomes the task of the minister of music to separate and remove the chaff and educate where necessary, utilizing music styles that in no way contradict the truth they portray. *Nowhere in Isaiah 6 (or elsewhere in Scripture) is the element of entertainment part of the worship experience.* The pleasure-rooted aspect of entertainment, although it has its place elsewhere, is inappropriate in the worship service. The removal of that single element from church services today would go a long way toward returning the church to its intended mission.

WORSHIP CAN BE LEARNED

Finally, the worship experience is taught—and learned—it does not just happen. The superficiality of experience is like the problem of the impoverished vocabulary—it is directly traceable to a deficiency in education. Much of the problem of lack of true worship stems from the fact that *very few people know how to worship.* A few years ago leaders who themselves had not learned to worship placed the blame for the problem on "irrelevant songs" or "stodgy old hymns." (Thankfully, in the purging process by those leaders some of the bad was discarded.) Hymns that had proved to be meaningfully effective for years were replaced by "here today, gone tomorrow" ditties that endeavored to accommodate the non-worshipers. Many churches discarded time-proved hymnals that previously lasted for years and replaced them with short-lived materials—almost like planned obsolescence! Even loose-leaf hymnbooks had to be developed because it was apparent that much of the new would not last. The new songs were going to solve everything. But did they? I submit that generally there are no more true worshipers as a result of the new song movement than before. Rather, there is a growing number of would-be worshipers who have unknowingly retooled the church into centers of entertainment and pleasure. Singers, choirs, and even pastors are applauded for their *performances*. The gimmicks of theatrical staging (all legitimate in the right place) have replaced the aura of the temple of God. In some churches taped orchestrations blandly accompany soloists and choirs in professional performances. Spotlights, sinking and rising platforms and pulpits, and waterfalls in the baptistry all contribute to the three-ringed, show-biz performances. People love it, but do they worship? When people are taught to worship they soon realize the emptiness of the entertainers' efforts and search for a church where their spiritual needs can indeed be met.

Worship can and should be taught in the church school. All too often children have been fed little musical ditties to fill time as the latecomers arrived prior to the important task of studying the Sunday school lesson. Yet, in recent years at least, they have had sophisticated materials for their church school lessons. The study of the Word has been rightfully stressed but the worship of God undermined. By implication, through music materials used, children were taught that the music experiences were unimportant, meaningless, and certainly irrelevant. What worship is, how the arts function in assisting in worship, and purposes of worship were not part of the experience. As the children grew up, they went through the motions of worship often with undue emphasis on the forms rather than the content. Seldom was it suggested that it is the worshiper who worships, not the forms or the music or the spoken word. However, when it is learned that *people* worship, that worship does not just happen but takes effort, that the total being is involved, and that worship is generally learned, then things begin to happen in the worship service. The craving for surface experience fades, people begin to demand authenticity, and the worship service is no longer a theatrical event but a vital, live encounter with God. The church no longer competes with the top Neilson-rated shows but becomes a unique entity in itself with a mission in the world that meets the deepest longing and needs of the human being. Happily, there is an increasing number of churches that are today rediscovering their mission in the world.

While there is valid subjectiveness to altar worship whereby something redemptive and spiritually creative is happening to the worshipper, it is nevertheless obvious that much of today's worship is almost entirely subjectively conceived. Too often it appears to be directed to the worshipper, concerned primarily with his personal gain and satisfactions, and seeking to influence his mental state. Its object is not the glory of God but the *experience* of the individual as a man-centered aim. There is nothing wrong with seeking emotional satisfaction or with desiring to be stirred to high resolves, but these motives unrestrained can become the sole rationale for church worship. It is by no means easy for us to learn that the center of attention in Christian worship is not the individual but God.*

> Oh, that I had a thousand voices
> To praise my God with thousand tongues!
> My heart, which in the Lord rejoices,
> Would then proclaim in grateful songs
> To all, wherever I might be,
> What great things God has done for me![†]
> (Johann Mentzer)

*Ibid.
[†]Copyright 1941 Concordia Publishing House. Used by permission.

PART 2
THE PARTICIPANTS IN CHURCH MUSIC

5

The Church Music Leaders

THE MINISTER OF MUSIC AND MINISTRY

In a vast number of churches the responsibilities of the minister of music are either assumed by a worship or music committee, a single individual such as the choir director or organist, or the pastor. In smaller churches where multiple staffing does not exist, the responsibilities should be assigned to a church committee (assuming appropriate membership qualifications), the choir director, or the organist. In multiple staff situations it is essential that one individual be charged with the music responsibility.

THE LEADER'S ROLE

The title *minister of music* is preferred over *choir director* or *director of music* because the title itself focuses on the very purpose of church music. The involvement of the performers and the congregation in the service music experiences should not be the same as for other music performances outside the church. It is, rather, the Body of Christ using the vehicle of music in experiences that are spiritual in nature and God-directed in focus, thus ministering to the needs of the people as a result. There is a sense in which the worshiper ministers to God in the act of worship. Therefore, the one charged with overseeing and providing leadership in all aspects of the church music program can and should be a *minister of music.* If for no other reason (and there are obviously other reasons), the title helps the congregation and the musicians to remember the purpose of church music and the calling of the church musicians.

RESPONSIBILITIES OF THE MINISTER OF MUSIC

The minister of music plans and administers the total music program of the church. Spiritual and musical maturity are both essential to assist him in decisions relating to policy matters, program development, and budgeting. In the interpersonal relationships between the minister of music and the participants in the music program, opportunities exist for spiritual counseling that require similar understandings to those common to the clergy. Thus there is considerable opportunity for one with this calling to not only minister through his music talents as a director, singer, or organist, but also in the one-to-one relationships.

Church music departments have often been called the war departments of the church. Too frequently insecure musicians hiding behind facades of artistic temperaments destroy any chance for the Spirit of God to work through them because of the resultant tensions. Jealousy is not uncommon among those whose responsibilities put them in front of people. Church musicians are not immune from the human characteristics that can render any Christian weak or ineffective. It is incumbent upon the minister of music to order his personal life so as to be without reproach. A constant dependency upon God's guidance through the Holy Spirit, careful, open, and honest relationships with others, and the avoidance of evil or the appearance of evil are all spiritual attributes for which the minister of music should strive. One leads by example, and where the example is inadequate so also will be both the leadership and the worship experiences of the followers. Regardless of one's musical expertise, true ministry only results from lives lived in conformity with God's will and from a dedicated commitment to Him. If any members of a church music staff are for any reason not part of the team effort in the ministering endeavor, it is the responsibility of the minister of music to approach such people in love and ultimately resolve the problems. In the best of situations interpersonal relationships can be occasionally strained, but if tensions persist, the ministry is bound to be hindered.

Because of the complexity of the relationships of the office as well as the confidentiality necessary in interpersonal relationships, I personally prefer one individual to be responsible rather than a committee. The ideal is to have one individual with the qualities, qualifications, and calling that will effectively provide the needed leadership. That individual should have freedom to select his staff members. When selecting staff members, the minister of music should look for team players who are not only effective musicians and spiritual leaders but whose perspectives are similar to those desired. Obviously one choir director who uses literature not in keeping with the basic music philosophy can undermine the program.

THE CONDUCTOR/CHOIR DIRECTOR

The conductor wears many hats during the course of his work. The selection of a music score, the analysis and study of the score, the initial presentation of the work to the choir, the correcting of mistakes, the development of a tonal production, the explanation of musical and textual ideas, the final polishing, and the actual conducting in performance all require a synthesis of his understanding in the areas of music literature, vocal techniques, conducting techniques, music history, group dynamics, music theory, and Scripture. The conductor must not only be a good musician, but he must be able to draw upon many different areas of knowledge to become proficient. The conductor is a leader not only of music but of people and as a result has the full responsibility for developing techniques that efficiently and effectively bring the desired results.

Ultimately the full responsibility for artistic or mediocre performance lies on the shoulders of the conductor. Leland Sateren, professor emeritus and conductor, Augsburg College Choir, Minneapolis, has said, "There is no such thing as poor choirs; there are only poor conductors!" It is true that the better the talent that exists within any given musical organization, the better the potential for excellence in performance.* But that potential can be realized only if the conductor is able to motivate and encourage the reaching of that potential. In many instances the talent has been average within performing groups, but because an outstanding conductor has worked with the group exceptional performance levels have been achieved. Ultimately the conductor cannot blame his singers (the bad little church choir or the untalented youth choir) for poor performance. Only incapable people blame others for their own inadequacies. The capable conductor assumes full responsibility for insuring excellence of performance.

*Refer to chapter 7 for a discussion of the place of excellence in the church music program.

THE CHALLENGE OF THE CHORAL CONDUCTOR

The conductor is a leader, not a follower. As a result it is important that he not only develop the techniques of leadership musically but also have some of the personality characteristics that set people apart as leaders in other areas of life as well. There are successful conductors who are also very quiet and in some ways unassuming or introverted. Generally speaking, however, the personality patterns for successful conductors tend to follow the extrovert kind of personality. Chances for success are somewhat less for one who tends to be shy and withdrawn than for one who tends to be outgoing and able to speak in front of people with some ease. That should not be construed to suggest that it is impossible for the shy person to be a successful conductor. It simply means that he may want to develop his personality through the taking of courses such as drama or public speaking, or through other means, in order to more comfortably become a leader.

The conductor is an accomplished musician. He must not only be a leader generally, but he must be a musical leader. The musical ear must be well developed so he can "hear" very easily (essentially an intellectual process). He must develop the mental capacity for perceiving notational error and be a good music reader. It would be absurd to assume that one who cannot read music could ever achieve at any significant level as a conductor. (Of course there have been a few exceptions.) Score reading becomes one of the primary responsibilities of the conductor, and teaching others to read is part of the task as well.

The conductor is a music historian. He must be totally aware of the styles of all the music periods. Because the conductor synthesizes music history and translates historical fact into his work, it is imperative that he develop an understanding of music history that gives rise to the sound of a given style. For example, the word *Baroque* must conjure up sounds for him, not merely names and dates. The conductor not only recognizes the Baroque style but creates it with live musicians from the musical and textual score. Interpretations are maximally the wishes of the composer (an accurate reading of the score) and must minimally be an extension of the conductor's own personality, feelings, or desires. The conductor is thus a servant of the score rather than the egotistical master of the score. Musically educated artist-conductors place themselves under the wishes of the composer. Everything is done within their power to interpret the score, always thinking of the wishes of the composer. Thus it is that the conductor must be steeped in the general characteristics of the style he is working with and the specific desires of the composer within that style. The self-indulgent conductor who specializes in an exclusively personal interpretation reflects an amateur point of view.

The conductor is a music theoretician. He must be able to analyze each score both harmonically and formally. Thematic development, understanding musical phrasing, and the shaping of line are important elements of that analysis in order that those music elements are apparent in performance.

The conductor is an aesthetician. He must know the aesthetic realm because he deals in the aesthetic realm with both the audience and his performers. He has views on the word *beauty*, on the arts as they relate to each other, on what music means, and on how to evaluate music. Thus he develops a philosophic frame of reference from which to work that will steer him in the selection of all literature performed with the given group or groups for which he is responsible.

The conductor knows the psychology of group dynamics. He must develop techniques of motivation to encourage responses to the musical gestures. It is important to anticipate singers' responses in rehearsal situations so that expectations for the group may be met. A rehearsal climate of artistic gratification and achievement is necessary to maintain the members in a choir, to assist in the recruiting process, and to insure good performance. The conductor is charged with maintaining good group morale, which necessitates an understanding of how to encourage positive interpersonal relationships within the group. The conductor must be aware of the psychological conditions that give rise to meaning in music so that performances reflect those considerations.

The conductor is a voice teacher. He must be able to develop good basic vocal habits on the part of the singers, solving their specific vocal problems. A basic vocal philosophy, which will give rise to all he does vocally and result in a specific "sound" of the choir, is necessary. We probably have all heard choirs the sound of which would be difficult to describe. When that is the case, one can be relatively certain that the conductor has not taught any specific vocal approach. On the other hand, the sound of the Roger Wagner Chorale, the Robert Shaw Chorale, Concordia, St. Olaf or Bethel Choirs, or the Johnny Mann Singers is easily recognized. The reason for that is that in each case the conductor has taught specific vocal approaches that resulted in a given sound for his group. It is at this point that the individual stamp of the conductor's personality and vocal philosophy is probably most apparent. His own creativity and understanding is most legitimately utilized in this manner.

By contrast, the interpretation of scores leaves much less room for individuality. It is far less legitimate for the personality of the conductor to be stamped on a piece of Bach than it is for the choir to employ a vocal philosophy that bears the stamp of the name of the conductor. Effective and pleasing singing does not just happen. It is taught through specific vocal exercises and an emphasis on a specific vocal production.

The conductor is an educator. Because so much time is spent teaching, it is necessary to develop sound pedagogical techniques. The conductor does not only teach specific notes and sounds, but he also teaches attitudes and concepts that must transfer from one musical situation to another. The ability to be a quick problem solver is necessary, and in being a problem solver he must often utilize pedagogical techniques that are effective.

The choral conductor is aware of the structure and meaning in the text of the literature to be performed. The text of every piece must be understood literally and poetically, and the conductor must be able to solve all problems of articulation and performance relating to the text as well as to the music. *Ideas* must be sung—not merely words.

The conductor is an administrator-organizer. He prepares budgets, organizes and plans schedules, files reports for those to whom he is responsible, and coordinates music activities with others of the music department and the institution at large (the school or the church). The choir is a complex organization, and the conductor must be highly efficient and organized so as to use time wisely.

He is also charged with the responsibility of determining how large numbers of people spend their time. If he has a rehearsal once a week or even one hour every day, multiplying that time by the number of members in the choir will give him the total number of hours for which he is directly responsible. Assuming he directs several choirs a week in rehearsal, the total number of hours for which the director is responsible is enormous. From a Christian perspective the stewardship of time is of as much importance as the stewardship of money. It therefore becomes imperative that time not be wasted in rehearsals. Humor has its place as a pacing device, but when rehearsals become joke-telling sessions or a waste in any other way, the conductor must be held directly accountable. The conductor soon learns that the greatest enemy to success is lack of time in rehearsal. As a result he must organize his thinking and plan rehearsals well so that as much as possible can be packed into each rehearsal.

The conductor is not only an artist-musician but also a master of the conducting technique. Through conducting gestures and other visual means, every aspect of the music must be expressed. The conductor is the eye-gate of both the performers and the congregation. Everything done must have meaning musically. The conductor must develop technique that reflects not only such things as good attacks, good breathing, line, releases, and fluid beat patterns but must do so within the context of the style of any of the periods conducted. In other words, he develops techniques that best reinforce the music to be conducted within the style of that music. That must be done within the boundaries of traditional conducting techniques so that as the conductor moves from one group to another it is not necessary to immediately teach what the gestures mean. The gestures must be so convincing that an untrained singer will respond automatically to them without having to ask for verbal explanation as to their meaning. And too, it is important that members of an accompanying orchestra or other instrumentalists clearly understand the conducting gestures so as to not waste precious rehearsal time. That is only achieved through the utilization of the traditional conducting gestures used by orchestral and formally educated choral conductors.

The conductor is never a showman. A conductor worthy of his calling must be a sincere, honest, deeply dedicated musician endeavoring to lead the performers in the creation of a meaningful experience. Thus *making the conducting gesture look like the music sounds* is necessary and should become the goal of all conducting students. Flamboyance and showmanship routines have no place in the concert hall of serious music and certainly are every bit as inappropriate in the church.

Finally, perhaps the single most important requirement of artist-conductors is that they provide meaningfully satisfying experiences for their congregation or audiences and the performers. The conductor who cannot do that is merely a mechanical musician going through the motions and leading performers in mechanical reproductions of the music. Within the context of church music, meaningful spiritual experiences are primary in importance, but artistic values also remain an important part of the total experience as well.

The effectiveness of the conductor will be determined by his ability to develop the varying responsibilities stated above and the ability to interrelate those responsibilities at a high level of achievement. Conductors will be stronger in some areas than others, but too much weakness in any single area will limit their overall effectiveness. The serious conductor's task, then, is to develop his abilities to the highest level. There are no shortcuts; success is only achieved through discipline and hard work. The practice necessary for success in conducting is exactly the same kind of practice necessary for success as a pianist, violinist, trombonist, vocalist, or other artist. Some think that all one has to do to become a conductor is to learn how to beat $^3/_4$ or $^4/_4$ patterns. (That, unfortunately, is how some church choir directors are chosen.) Anyone who views conducting in that manner simply does not understand the role of the conductor. Conductors who are artist-conductors have worked at the perfection of their art in precisely the same way the great artists in other fields have done. That means daily practice of technique and the development of musicianship until each is mastered. At the point at which technique and musicianship are mastered and he has developed a broad repertoire of technique, the conductor then spends time selecting and studying scores in precisely the same way any accomplished artist studies his work.

It is possible for one not to have a strong conducting technique and still develop a good level of performance. In such cases, however, performance of the music must be in a mechanical fashion because the conductor would not dare change anything in performance for fear the performers would not know what such a change in gesture would mean. Inspiration in the moment of performance is held in check because the conductor is forced to recreate exactly what he has done in each of the preceding rehearsals.

Some of the most meaningful experiences choirs and audiences have are when the performance issues in a level of communication that comes through the excitement of on-the-spot inspiration. Slight and subtle variations in the recreative act are only possible when the music is mastered by the choir and the conductor has the technique to respond to those moments of inspiration. A conductor incapable of going beyond mechanical reproduction really does not need more than minimal rehearsal time in preparation for each anthem. In churches where one hour per week is scheduled for preparation for Sunday services, that kind of restricted schedule is probably enough because in all likelihood the choir will simply "get by" anyway. But where conductors are capable of producing at much higher levels, adequate time to insure arriving at those levels is necessary. A good conductor who can produce at a high level will always take steps to assure adequate preparation for such production.

PERSONAL ATTRIBUTES COMMON TO SUCCESSFUL CONDUCTORS

Although it is unrealistic to think that every church has or will have artist-conductors as part of their church music programs, it is helpful to have goals for which aspiring young musicians may aim. Serious conductors in church music who are not satisifed with their present achievements and wish to improve their abilities and effectiveness can benefit from observation of those who are successful in the field. Through years of observation and discussion with eminently successful conductors I have discovered the following attributes to be apparent in those who were particularly successful. My observations have ranged from the most esteemed orchestral and choral conductors in the world to those who are effectively ministering in local churches in this country. They all seem to have several characteristics in common.

They have confidence in their professional endeavors. They know they are capable because of the repertoire of success they have built along the way. They are not necessarily proud (confidence and pride are two different characteristics). They tend to be outgoing in personality and have winsome ways.

They all demand excellence of performance from their performers. Their expectations are always high, and they keep self-discipline and hard work as the path to success. Mediocrity is born out of complacent self-satisfaction or a willingness to accept less than the best from a given group. Weak musicianship, weak leadership ability, weak conducting technique, laziness, or other reasons can be given for such mediocrity. However, successful artists are intolerant of mediocrity because of an *inner compulsion* to excel in their work. The demands made upon others are also made upon themselves. Average conductors who accept less than the best from their performers often do not know the difference between average and outstanding performance themselves. Thus it is that a group that performs for such a conductor is doomed to average or mediocre performance—an unfortunate waste of time and talent for the performers. Performers have a right to, and should in fact expect, the highest possible levels of achievement from their conductors.*

---

*Attitudes that foster mediocrity contribute largely to mediocre performances. It is incongruous to give less than one's best to the Lord. One must do his best not only to achieve a high artistic level but to honor God to the fullest of his ability. Pastors and administrators should know the difference between mediocre and outstanding performances and be committed to utilizing musicians who qualify.

They are able to envision the outcome long before the performance. Not only can they conceptualize the perfect performance in advance, but they can successfully bring their performers to a realization of that conceptualization. "What will be will be" or "let's see where we come out" attitudes simply do not exist among artists. They set goals and achieve those goals at all costs. Often the goals set are above what might be expected for a given group, but it is not uncommon for such groups to perform over their heads because of the effectiveness of the conductor. It is seldom if ever possible that a group will perform over its head when it has a conductor who has not aspired to such heights. More common is the situation in which the choir performs far below its ability and is hampered by its conductor.

They are never satisfied with their own performance or that of their performers. They always strive to grow and improve. They are driven by an inner sense that they can improve, and they take whatever steps are necessary to insure personal and group growth. They study music and scores for their entire lives to produce the desired musical excellence. The same compulsion produces a need for Christian conductors to study God's Word as well in order to produce the needed spiritual discernment. In the secular-realm, prior to his death, Arturo Toscanini was known to have been studying and working to improve in his work. Eminent conductors such as Leonard Bernstein, Herbert Von Karajan, Erich Leinsdorf, and Sir Georg Solti all set aside specific periods of time during the day when they work and adequately prepare themselves for their responsibilities. They know that there are no shortcuts to excellence. Hard work on the part of all (performers and conductor) is the only path to success. Practice is the *only* exercise that makes perfect. If the giants in the field must prepare themselves for providing great aesthetic experiences for those who hear them perform, it is every bit as important that those who minister in the name of the Lord be as well prepared in the utilization of music for spiritual ministry.

They are motivated primarily by the music demands rather than the social demands of the group. Their primary dedication is to the art of music and, within the realm of church music, spiritual communication. They are secondarily motivated to be dedicated to their performers. That does not mean that they are not loving and understanding and do not relate well to their performers. However, the *totally* people-centered conductor tends to specialize in the social interactions in the rehearsals and in the other personal contacts with the performers rather than on those interactions that are music-centered. Conversely, the music-centered conductor focuses his attention on the musical aspects of learning, mastering and performing the score. It is important that such a conductor not fall into the trap common to some otherwise successful conductors of viewing their performers only as performers. It must be remembered that the performers are people with feelings, who need the personal attention of the conductor. They are each important to the total success of the group. They may need encouragement and other forms of personal attention, all of which demand the time and energy of the conductor, who must strive to meet those needs. The rich experiences that can result from the give and take between conductor and performers should never be overlooked. The only factor that will limit such experiences will be the time that is consumed in so doing. The conductor will often feel a tension between his music responsibilities and social responsibilities to the group. Those social responsibilities must not become means in themselves (in the thinking of the conductor) lest choir members begin to enjoy being part of the group for reasons other than the musical/spiritual ones. When members begin to feel that it is a pleasure to be part of a group because of the benefits of group involvement or travel experiences (touring, fun on the buses, getting to know girls and boys) the conductor has moved from the realm of being a conductor to that of being a sociologist. The greatest compliment that can be paid to a conductor is that people want to *sing* for him because of the musical/spiritual experiences he provides. And more important, effective communication can take place through choirs' singing because they paid the price of mastering the music. Without a doubt the Holy Spirit uses people in spite of their inadequacies, but that is no reason to continue presumptively in inadequate music performance. The social aspects of the choir situation are important and need to be considered as such by the conductor. However, the successful conductor always focuses primarily on the musical responsibilities of the group.

THE ORGANIST

THE CHALLENGE OF THE CHURCH ORGANIST

The church organist is one of the most important leaders in the corporate service experience. The organist not only must be technically proficient on the instrument but thoroughly knowledgeable in the philosophic realm of church music. A poor organist can severely diminish effective potential of any service, and a good organist conversely can do wonders in insuring such potential. To technically master the instrument is only part of the task of the organist. An understanding of all service objectives (as well as being a sympathetic supporter of the objectives); a knowledge of organ literature (as literature to be used not for concert performance but as a utilitarian spiritual experience vehicle); a thorough awareness of purposes and implementation techniques for effective preludes, offertories, and postludes; a fundamentally sound accompanying ability; and the willingness to be a supportive and cooperative member of the music team (where the organist is not also the minister of music) are all necessary attributes for the effective organist. Again, the demands of the church music responsibility require more than the mastery of an instrument, as may more likely be the case of the concert artist. In addition, it is essential that the organist not only be sympathetic with the denominational implications of a church, but he must also have the necessary spiritual commitment and discernment that gives purpose and direction to his work. It is most unfortunate that some churches have been caught in the trap of employing organists whose only qualifications are skills related to the playing of the instrument. That may be due to the church's lack of understanding, vision, or willingness to appropriately fund the position, to an inadequate instrument, or to the unavailability of a fully qualified organist.

The organist, like the minister of music and the choir, leads the congregation in the important experience of congregational song. Harmonic or improvisatory creativity appropriate to the purposes of the service as well as within the context of the hymns can be a large asset in encouraging congregational involvement. That ability is perhaps a rare gift but is so helpful when used meaningfully by the organist. Most Christians have experienced those occasions when the introduction to the hymn was so much in context with the basic thrust of the hymn that they were compelled to sing with all of their being. There are also those experiences where the organist was more effective at turning off the congregation than at encouraging them. Thus it is that the task of the organist is not only to play the instrument effectively but to lead the congregation.

THE SELECTION OF SERVICE LITERATURE

Usually the organist's responsibilities in literature selection are limited to the prelude, offertory, and postlude sections of the service. To haphazardly select pieces is to miss the total potential for spiritual experience during those moments. Generally speaking, it is a rare organist who is not conscientious in his responsibilities. Organists who have studied the instrument not only for the purpose of being concert artists but also to primarily function as church organists are usually exemplary in that regard.

The prelude. The purpose of the prelude is to prepare people (after they have entered the sanctuary) for the experience of worship. It is in fact the beginning of spiritual involvement of the worshiper rather than a perfunctory aural experience at the beginning of the service. It is not music "to walk in to" or "to socialize to." Where it is thus used, the pastor and minister of music have an education job to do. More will be needed than the usual impotent heading in the bulletin exhorting all to be silent and bow their heads in meditation and prayer. It is also not a mini-concert for the organist to demonstrate his skill on the pedals. When the congregation fully understands the purpose of the prelude, and the literature played convincingly supports that purpose, the people will usually respond appropriately. The task can be made more difficult by architectual aspects of the sanctuary. When people enter a sanctuary they bring with them all of the burdens and tensions and a multitude of extraneous aspects of life that must be consciously quieted in order to get seriously involved in the act of worship. Some sanctuaries visually reinforce a sense of respect, awe, and seriousness of purpose upon entering. Others, however, may reflect an opposite atmosphere—one that is almost flippant or irreverant. In such edifices the organist's task is much more difficult and in some cases, perhaps impossible. If what the ears hear is not reinforced by what the eyes see, the chances of effective involvement are diminished. Certainly, a congregation that worships in such an environment does so in spite of the situation and without the helps and aids that can be so meaningful in encouraging the appropriate responses.

Architectural considerations aside, the prelude should always be chosen with two things in mind. First, the objectives of the experiences to follow, including the church calendar or seasonal thrusts. Second, an understanding of *what music means*—the selecting of pieces that create the desired basic moods and feelings and meanings that are supportive of the specific objectives. If worshipers are to use prayer to prepare themselves for worship, a bombastic, joyful, driving selection may not encourage the desired prayer involvement. If meditation is the objective, a meditative or pastoral setting is necessary. Organists simply cannot select literature because it is what they like, or what they feel like playing this week, or because it is by their favorite composer. When those are the criteria, their contributions will be relegated to the "unimportant" category in the minds of the congregation. But when the necessary time is spent in a careful and prayerful selection of the prelude, it can start the service in a meaningful direction.

The offertory. It is often the responsibility of the organist to play the offertory in churches where offertory solos or choir selections are not used. The purpose of the offertory is *not* to play background music while offering plates are being passed. The offertory should accomplish one or more of the following objectives:

1. It should provide a conscious corporate focus on the act of Christian stewardship. That can be done by playing a familiar hymn with a text that deals with the stewardship of time, talents, life, or money. It does not mean the organist should play *We Give Thee But Thine Own* each week. However, a periodic reference to the stewardship theme through a familiar hymn text is helpful.
2. It should create a mood conducive to non-corporate creative meditation by playing appropriate selections without familiar texts or with no text. Obviously there is no guarantee that the congregation will use this time appropriately. They must be taught to utilize such moments, and there is great risk for non-involvement. Such risk is acceptable, however, because as a congregation grows in its understanding and commitment to genuine worship, moments that can be uniquely individualized become increasingly precious. The insecure worshiper will always want each time slot filled by an activity in which he is led. The worshiper who is willing or even desirous to exert extra energy in the worship experience will inevitably appreciate moments set aside for non-corporate meditation.
3. It should focus attention on the broader themes of the service. (But at some point, either through congregational singing and/or verbal corporate prayer, the act of stewardship in worship must come into focus.)

The offering and offertory is not a time for relaxation on the part of the congregation (either physically or mentally) but an important time of spiritual dedication and giving—a time that must be carefully thought through by the one who provides the appropriate musical leadership.

Background prayer music. In some churches it is common for the organist to play while the pastor leads the congregation in prayer. Often this is done at the beginning or end of the offering when the ushers come forward. The organist may also be requested to play background music during the pastoral prayer. The origin of this practice is not well documented—perhaps it began in churches who broadcast their services on radio and had to provide "filler" for the radio audience. At any rate, organists and pastors alike need to know that when something familiar is played while a prayer is offered, the minds of the congregation will often, and perhaps usually, gravitate to the text or tune of the familiar hymn rather than pray with the pastor. For the less disciplined they may even *only* mentally hum the tune with no conscious involvement in the prayer. Further, there can be ridiculous incongruity between the thoughts of the prayer and what is played.

It sometimes seems that some pastors must hate silence because during moments of silent prayer they also request the organist to play background music—once again like a radio program. If the text is familiar, the pastor may as well audibly read the text because the attention of the congregation is occupied in mentally following the music and text of what is played. Creative non-corporate prayer (where heaven is bombarded with as many different prayers as there are worshipers in the church) can only take place when there are no musical sounds to distract the worshiper. Some may feel that background music makes the worship service smoother. If one were to view the service within the context of a radio program that might be true. But as an aid to worship it flunks the test. The organist in such a situation would do well to tactfully encourage the pastor not to expect background music during prayers. If music must be provided during silent prayers, it must be understood that no one will pray a prayer other than the text related to the music that is being played by the organist (assuming it is familiar). Organists who try to avoid playing familiar hymns, knowing full well what happens to the congregation, may then begin to improvise, and if they are not extremely gifted, such improvisation can also detract from the worship experience. The point is that if music is to be used during any prayer time, it must be very carefully thought out so that it is supportive rather than damaging to the prayer experience. It is a curious thing that some pastors prefer music with their prayers, which creates a kind of competition for the attention of the worshiper. In most cases the music wins out.

The postlude. Too often it could be tempting for the organist to select the postlude in isolation from the specific thrust of the service. Unfortunately, the postlude becomes concert time for some organists. But the time is abused not only by organists; congregations also misuse the postlude. They use the postlude as "walking out music," to loudly greet friends, or for general socializing. But the postlude is not background music for socializing. The congregation has a valid need to socialize and greet one another following the service. A friendly welcome to visitors and happy social interaction among believers is not only desired but should be strongly encouraged—following the postlude, not during it. Where no foyer exists, and the church is so designed that there is no space other than the sanctuary for this purpose, it admittedly becomes a difficult problem. One solution is that the congregation remain in place until the postlude is completed. Ideally the postlude is a musical culmination of the final thrust of the service (often articulated in the sermon), creating the intellectual (cognitive) and emotional (affective) conclusions appropriate to the service. If the final thrust is one of *joy* the postlude should be appropriately happy. If it is *dedication* to the task of serving the Lord, it ought to reflect a sense of determination and boldness. In some circumstances silence may be an appropriate response, but happy people may desire to respond overtly during the postlude.

Where the organist does not coordinate preludes, offertories, and postludes with the objectives and themes of the service, precious time is wasted, and in essence the idea that those moments are unimportant is unwittingly signaled. When the organist conscientiously does endeavor to choose appropriate selections, it then becomes the responsibility of the pastor, minister of music, and others who can help to encourage and teach the congregation to use the time wisely. The conscientious organist always checks with the pastor to ascertain the primary thrust of the sermon. The postlude is then selected and scheduled so as to support the mood and emotions of that thrust.

CORPORATE AND NON-CORPORATE EXPERIENCES

It is important for the organist to understand how corporate experiences differ from non-corporate experiences because the organist involves the congregation in both group and creative individualized thought patterns. Any selection chosen with a text or title familiar to the congregation evokes responses that follow in the direction of that text or title. When *What a Friend We Have in Jesus* is played, in most churches the text conjures up meanings, feelings, emotions, and total corporate responses that are limited to the context of that text. If what is desired is a singular kind of experience that is less creative on the part of the worshiper, that kind of selection is appropriate. However, when what is desired is a non-corporate freedom that encourages individual creativity of thought and involvement, one must not restrict the congregation with such a selection. Rather, the organist should choose literature with no text at all or at least with an unfamiliar text. With that type of music the focus more consciously shifts to the moods and abstract feelings that are created by the selection. It is precisely for such non-corporate reasons that Bach, Buxtehude, Franck, or other composers of organ music are used in services. Obviously the congregation has to know how to use such literature, or the organist will frequently hear "he never plays anything I know!" Such statements are an indication that the individual does not understand the purpose of the prelude or the exciting potential of the creative non-corporate experience. Again education and encouragement are the answer. Organists who only play Bach because it is great music or because he happens to be their favorite composer are in need of education themselves. A congregation usually reflects the effectiveness of its leadership in its understandings. Organists who blame congregations for lack of understanding or involvement often need to point the finger of blame at themselves. However, the organist cannot do the job of education alone. It is up to the minister of music and pastor to reinforce a correct vision in these directions and so assist the organist in his work.

THE ORGANIST'S INSTRUMENT

The reason some churches have difficulty employing gifted and qualified organists is sometimes due to the fact that the church organ is so inadequate. As it is impossible to make a silk purse out of a sow's ear, so it is also impossible for a bad organ to effectively function as an instrument of worship. Small churches with limited resources may be pressed to install no more than an adequate instrument. When funds cannot specifically accommodate a good pipe organ, some of the newer electronic instruments are a good solution.

The design of the sanctuary and the acoustics of the church all have an impact on how an instrument will sound. As with vocal music, hard surfaces reinforce and enhance the sound of the organ. Soft absorbent surfaces deaden the sound, not only playing havoc with the vocal production of the choir but with the sound of the organ as well. Church leaders preoccupied with carpeting, soft seats on the pews, and other sound absorbent materials would do well to visit the cathedrals of Europe. The churches of the world with incredible acoustics are the ones where no carpet, draperies, or sound absorbent materials exist. A fine instrument in poor acoustics will not be effective. Therefore the congregation concerned about realizing the optimum potential of the organ (and I might add—the choir) must be equally concerned about the acoustics of the church as they are about the instrument that is installed.

Although it is desirable, it is not essential to have a recital-quality instrument in a church. If the primary purpose of the use of the organ is kept in mind, the church will insure that an organ is selected that can effectively enhance the congregational singing, accompany the choir and soloists, and play appropriate prelude and postlude literature. My opinion is that it is better to install a more limited pipe organ than a more elaborate electronic instrument.

Some electronic instruments come close to imitating pipe organ sounds, but in my judgment there still is no substitute for the genuine product. To date, I have heard many electronic instruments (some very elaborate and costly), but none compare to the good pipe organs I have heard throughout the world. Generally, a good pipe organ outlives the electronic instrument and is probably a better long-term investment for the church. Contrary to what one hears from enthusiastic electronic fans, the pipe organ is not necessarily a great deal more expensive to maintain than an electronic organ. If a budget is extremely limited, the electronic instrument may be the solution. Most important, this aspect of the budgetary philosophy of the church deserves careful consideration and insight that penetrates beyond the immediate future. The difference between a poor electronic instrument and a small but effective pipe organ can mean a radical difference in how the congregation worships in each service.

Thankfully, few churches install electronic organs of the bar room or roller-and-ice-skating-rink variety anymore. And too, the reputable electronic companies usually encourage churches to steer away from their theater or one-man-band models. Dollars spent (albeit sacrificially) on excellent instruments are dollars invested in the future worship life of the congregation and become not an investment in a keyboard, pipes, and air source, but in lives.

6

The Church Musicians

THE CHOIR MEMBER

COMMITMENT OF THE SINGER

Some of the nicest people in the world are the ones who sit in choir lofts at eleven o'clock each Sunday. Very often they are not only choir members but church school teachers, deacons, church board members, members of worship committees or missions groups, or they may have any number of other church responsibilities. Outside of church obligations they are often professional people, executives, homemakers, or those active in community affairs. They are usually busy people with talents dedicated to serving the Lord. What a privilege musicians have in working with such servants! Often multiple-talented, they are evidence that talent invested in the Lord's work grows and flourishes.

It is essential that the minister of music recognize the importance of each individual in the choir. To be sure, some have better voices than others, but faithfulness to the tasks of the choir is the most important ingredient for an effective ministry. In recruiting members, the director should communicate that requisite and avoid members who cannot be faithful. Faithfulness to a church choir's ministry is impossible unless there is first a spiritual commitment to the Lord and His work. Commitment to the church is not enough. Although the members themselves may reflect differing levels of spiritual understanding and maturity, they should all qualify for the choir by their desire to use their voices to glorify God. The pleasures derived from singing great choral music or simply the joy of singing should be viewed as secondary reasons for involvement in a church choir. Community choruses exist for those whose commitments focus more readily on such purposes.

COMMITMENT OF THE DIRECTOR

Choir members have the right to expect total preparation from their director at all rehearsals. Directors who complain that their members are unfaithful in rehearsal attendance would do well to analyze their own techniques and effectiveness. Assuming concurrence as to primary objectives and requirements for choir membership, the director who produces at a high level with a well-paced rehearsal will have little trouble with rehearsal attendance. When problems occur it is an indication of either a lack of dedication on the part of the singer or ineffective leadership by the director. Some directors use rehearsal time to tell stories, jokes, or simply to talk. Humor is an excellent pacing device, but people generally resent their time being wasted by a talker or a stand-up comedian. Talking about how to perform the music, aside from some text explanations, reflects a weak conducting technique. Every precious minute should be used in constructive and productive rehearsal with enough spiritual and musical gratification in evidence to make the singers *look forward to rehearsals*. Boring rehearsals and performances result in attendance problems.

THE REHEARSAL SCHEDULE

Although the director must use the rehearsal time wisely, it is imperative that the choir rehearsals be scheduled with adequate time to insure that the choir can be effective and successful in its task. Some churches guarantee failure from the start by placing a low priority on the rehearsal schedule. Scheduling rehearsals after midweek prayer services or Bible studies guarantees late starts and tired singers. Singers cannot be expected to place high priority on their attendance and contribution when it is obvious that they get the leftovers in the schedule. To ask a choir to step into the pulpit unprepared each Sunday to lead a congregation in worship is a travesty. Churches will not tolerate a pastor to so prepare each week yet may frequently allow schedule restrictions that guarantee marginal success at best from the choir. Singers themselves become frustrated because they may be committed to a give-God-your-best philosophy but cannot possibly realize such a goal from the church choir. I prefer a separate night for choir rehearsal because those who participate in midweek services usually do so anyway even though the choir is on a separate night. Sometimes choices have to be made that eliminate individuals from one or the other, but it is essential that the choir rehearsal time be a protected time and long enough to guarantee effective preparation.

A good solution to the midweek service-choir rehearsal dilemma is to have a devotional in the choir rehearsal. Such moments are helpful for the choir's spiritual involvement, and the moments of study and/or prayer are moments that produce rich dividends in the lives of the members and director. Spiritual food from the Word as well as frequent communication with God is necessary in the church choir situation to cement a group together and focus their minds and hearts on their primary objective.

SUGGESTED GUIDELINES FOR CHOIR MEMBERSHIP

Regardless of the size of the church or choir, rules for membership serve as unifying factors to reinforce the stated objectives of the group. From the time I first directed my church choir at age nineteen I have had precise and clearly defined guidelines for membership. They include the following:

1. Attendance at rehearsals and at services at which the choir sings is required. The choir rehearses a minimum of three weeks on each anthem sung, and a member must have been in attendance two of the three weeks in order to sing the given anthem. Nothing is worse for morale or choral effectiveness than to have singers miss rehearsals and then come in and "botch things up" in the service. *No one* is so good that he can be allowed to transgress this ruling.
2. More than three unexcused absences suggests a priority problem for the singer, and he is counseled to reconsider his commitment or withdraw from the choir.
3. Excused absences include illness, death in the family, business trips, and vacations. If business requirements result in more than ten total absences from rehearsals and services, the singer is asked to reconsider his commitment. Thus an occasional business trip is acceptable; frequent ones are not.
4. Tardiness (except for reasonable excuses) is not acceptable. The director must begin and end rehearsals on time as a commitment to the singers. In addition, tardiness is disruptive to the rehearsal. There are often a few who are undisciplined in punctuality, and they must be encouraged to resolve

that problem so as to not disrupt the rehearsal with late entrances. Stressing the importance of each individual to the whole helps people realize that they are *all* needed to start a rehearsal. In tardiness as in absences the director must be open and accepting in reasonable situations but firm and unaccepting of undisciplined punctuality or erratic attendance.

5. Singers who know of a future absence such as travel are expected to notify the director in advance. Otherwise, all absences are to be phoned into the church office with a reason for the absence left for the director prior to the rehearsal or service. It is important for the director to know about absences so as to make ensemble adjustments in the anthem. When the singers recognize that they cannot slide between the cracks (regardless of the size of the choir), but that they are indeed important to the choir's total ministry, they then will hopefully assume the full obligation of effective membership.

In my choirs if problems persist, I try to win the individual over through the year. Anyone who has not proven himself to be faithful by the end of the year is not invited to return the next year. I am convinced it is far better to have a small choir of faithful members than a large one that includes unfaithful ones.

THE SOLOISTS

QUALIFICATIONS OF SOLOISTS

Those who are blessed with unusual gifts should be used in the church as soloists (or in ensembles) when appropriate occasions arise. It is necessary that the soloist not only be properly motivated, having the sincere desire to use his voice to lead the congregation and glorify God, but also have a special vocal gift. Occasionally there are those in churches whose own perspective of their vocal ability differs from that of the music leader. It may be that in earlier years an individual had a beautiful solo voice, but perhaps with age the voice has changed. Or it may be that an individual does not have an accurate impression of his own vocal ability. It is unfortunate that individuals are asked to sing when in fact they do not have the vocal ability to lead the congregation in genuine worship. In years past I recall hearing soloists with such vibratos or intonation problems that by the time they were through my hands would be wringing wet from the anxiety that was created. My response was not that of a fussy musician but common to many in the congregation. Often one would hear the comment that the soloist's "heart was right" as if a right heart were all that was necessary to lead a congregation. Certainly a right heart is necessary, but the vocal dimension is also important. Soloists are sometimes chosen for political reasons—the individual may be influential in the church, or a favorite son or daughter, or maybe the pastor's wife. Again such short-sighted and insincere motivation for solo singing is out of place.

It is also not uncommon in some churches for individuals to be used who have a great talent but whose lives and/or motives do not reinforce the message that they sing. Although they may be professional musically, the element of Spirit-guided communication can be lost. Professionalism without a ministry orientation in church music may produce recital-type (aesthetic) responses that are inappropriate to the objectives of the worship service. In the former situation there is sincere motivation with an absence of excellence, and in the latter there is excellence with an absence of proper motivation. In both instances solo singing will be found lacking.

Of course the ideal to strive for is the involvement of talented musicians who are dedicated to the spiritual values of the music ministry. For effective communication to take place, one has to be sufficiently gifted so as to get out of the way of the message. Bad tonal production or poor intonation interferes with the message. The Spirit can and often does bless in spite of the singer, but responsible church musicians must endeavor to select those who can best lead in spiritual experiences.

MINISTRY AND THE SOLOIST

One of the responsibilities of the minister of music is to help train and educate soloists both in talent development and literature selection. All literature sung should be appropriate to service themes and be consistent in both textual and musical meanings. Because so many of today's singers (particularly young musicians) model themselves both vocally and in their performance mannerisms after pop artists, the minister of music needs to assist in steering them in more appropriate directions (not all of what they have learned is inappropriate). A sense of confidence and visual (not overdone) expressions supportive of the text are appropriate positive performance aspects. However, anything done that promotes or points to the singer is out of place. Because the pop music business is essentially an entertainment business, techniques are used to reflect the greatness of the artist. In order to sell records the public has to be impressed with the individual as much as with the individual's song. There is constant concern with the performers image. Staging, choreography, and all sorts of visual gimmicks are used to sell the singer.

In church music the focus needs to be away from the musician and on the message. Performance techniques are only appropriate when they enhance the message rather than the singer, and the singer is really the insignificant one who has simply delivered the message. No ego trips are appropriate. Sincerity is easily evaluated in short order because self-promoters are obvious. Not all singers who use "show biz techniques" realize the inappropriateness of their performance styles. The mass media generation often knows nothing more than such approaches and sincerely uses them, thinking they are doing their best for God. The church musician does well to tactfully encourage and steer so as to not hurt such an individual. But when and where such singers are used requires strength of conviction and wisdom so as to not sell the worship experience short. Individuals are important, but God's work must have a higher priority. It must be remembered that people ideally do not go to church to be entertained or see a live television show. Soloists or musicians who want to be entertainers should be encouraged to entertain in an appropriate environment and circumstance.

There is nothing wrong with clean entertainment. Good pop music is enjoyable and not at odds with the Spirit-filled life. What is at odds is the inability of some to discriminate as to appropriateness of time, place, and usage. Some churches have created their own problems by trying to rule out all forms of entertainment as sinful. Because some folksongs have double entendres or texts that are suggestive, they frown on listening to all pop music. Such church leaders think they do away with the whole problem by singing "sacred texts" to the same music styles. They in fact entertain themselves with entertainment music styles but have purified the textual content. They can have spiritual texts and yet get their "kicks" at the same time. How much better it is to teach discriminatory entertainment using the entertainment styles as intended and using different styles when involved in the communication of spiritual truth. The house of God must be reserved for the unique experiences that are not reminiscent of the nightclub act or variety stage show. Where church leaders err in this regard, they are probably not fully aware of the incongruities created or are not spiritually tuned in to the biblical focus of spiritual experience.

APPROPRIATE LITERATURE

To use biblical texts as entertainment is in itself a dead giveaway as to the view held of Scripture. To those who see Scripture as good literature it is not a distant step to make light of its content by having fun with it (entertainment orientation). To those who view Scripture as the Word of God with the only revelation to man of God's forgiveness and saving grace, there is little room for it to be couched in a cheap commercial or entertaining language. As mentioned in an earlier chapter, selling Jesus Christ like sex or toothpaste is more than slightly incongruous. Christian radio stations who unwittingly help create the entertainment syndrome are partly at fault. But the penetration of that approach into church solo and choral literature is the fault of ministers of music who make the decision to use such singers and literature.

TALENT DEVELOPMENT

Although the church music leadership and the church have the responsibility to encourage the growth and maturation of the budding musician in the church, the worship service is not necessarily the place to break them in. Youth services, camp services, banquets, services of evangelism, nursing home services, and informal gatherings provide opportunities for the young and/or developing talent to be used. The worship service should be reserved for the use of talent that is seasoned and effective so as to have the best potential for leading the congregation in spiritual experience. There will be pressures to use "Suzie" or "Johnnie," but a place should be found for them to serve in appropriate services.

The apprenticeship concept is a good one to employ in the development and encouragement of talent. The church that has no opportunities to use young and developing talents will lose such individuals from the church to other performance avenues. Some churches with a strong vision as to their responsibility in those areas have music schools offering private lessons to their membership. That trend will undoubtedly grow as budgets are cut in public schools and music opportunities decrease. The more opportunities the church can create for the talented young, the better the chances for a strong future music program as well as for the young people realizing their full musical potential. Where spiritual values can be taught along with the music lesson, proper patterns can be established early in life and God-given talents nourished in Christ-centered directions.

A WORD ABOUT THE USE OF NEW CHRISTIANS

There has been a trend in recent years for some churches to use big name entertainers who have come to Christ. Needless to say, there is rejoicing here and in heaven when anyone accepts God's gift of salvation, and the church must find ways to encourage and involve such new believers. The basic problem however, is that when a known pop artist is used, the individual becomes an overnight hero in the Christian community and is catapulted into a place of spiritual leadership far before spiritual maturity is in evidence.

It is a strange phenomenon—entertainment-hungry Christians flocking to hear this rock group or that pop singer who is now "one of them." Christian record companies cater to such Christians and market the pop singers through the Christian radio stations and recordings. The influence that that well-orchestrated commercial venture has produced in church music is enormous. The young people in particular often want the top forty tunes of the Christian charts to be used in their churches. In some ways the influence of that stage show mentality has been greater in certain church music circles than probably any other single factor. It is not the result of chance but is the work of a number of profiteers with a clearly delineated strategy in the "sacred" pop music business. The coalition between some music publishers and recording companies has effectively produced the dilemma.

The problem is twofold: singers whose best abilities are entrenched in show business become "spiritual leaders" through their music, and music becomes more entertainment-oriented than spiritually-oriented. The texts are often acceptable (although usually highly personalized or subjective), but the vocal style, arrangements, music styles, and often the life-styles of the singers themselves are all the same as in their pre-Christian days. Young people choose those stars as models and carefully imitate them. Seldom does one hear a young person sing a gospel or sacred song in a style other than the entertaining (sometimes even seductive) styles. It is a short step for the church to move from centers of profound spiritual experience to entertainment centers with quasi-religious overtones as the church of tomorrow is led by such individuals. Voice teachers in serious Christian institutions are in a quandary because young singers no longer wish to seriously develop their vocal talents. There is little reason for them to do so when they discover they can sing like the stars, with no formal study at all. The church has been burned in other areas by thrusting new converts into the forefront of leadership before it was time. Leaders in church music would do well to encourage young talent but also to gently steer it in directions more suitable to church music objectives.

THE INSTRUMENTALISTS

PURPOSES IN INSTRUMENTAL MUSIC

Instrumental music in the church can add much to the music program if its purpose is understood and the instrumentalists have guidance. Very often an instrumentalist is asked to play a special number or offertory, but little is said in steering the performer in directions appropriate for the service.

I recall as a Bible school student being asked to play for church services as a member of a trumpet trio. We played fancy arrangements, triple tonguing wherever possible, and in general wailing away with every insincere motivation. Friends in school thought we were great (although some of the music faculty must have had other ideas). Churches invited us back, and we were sent around to perform at youth rallies. With maturity, I realized we had been nothing short of entertainers. Rather than the stage or night club circuit, ours was the church circuit. Sadly, no one ever explained to us what the purpose of our playing should have been. We learned by imitating the then current pop artists. If someone had tried to help us, we might not have listened. But the seed of truth might have been planted, and I might have got turned around sooner than I did. Yes, we prayed before each service; we knew and used all the buzz words. We were probably sincere in wanting God to receive honor from our efforts, but we still did "our thing" when we played. Our youthful immaturity was probably normal. But it is important to note that no one stepped forward to challenge our approach. Even today, there are few who challenge the obvious insincerity encountered in church music circles.

Unless the situation is a concert, the purpose of instrumental music in the church is (as with all other music) to lead the congregation in a spiritual experience. That can be done using techniques that evoke either corporate or non-corporate responses, but those techniques must also reflect appropriate stylistic understandings.

CORPORATE INVOLVEMENT—PLAYING THE TEXT

The only way an instrumentalist can play a piece that leads the congregation in a singular direction is to play a selection the text of which is familiar or available to the congregation. A familiar hymn or gospel song can bring about spiritual insight as the text is followed. The instrumentalist must in such cases think the text as he plays, so as to interpret it appropriately. "Playing a text" is foreign to many instrumentalists because their training does not include that skill. Bands and orchestras do not play texts unless accompanying a choir and then they seldom are aware of the text, and solo literature is textless. Thus the average church instrumentalist performs a piece thinking only of the musical nuances and therefore possibly using a tonal style or tonguing/phrasing technique totally out of keeping with the message of the piece. The selection simply becomes another tune, neither sacred nor secular (notes in themselves are neither), that is played for the enjoyment (aesthetic ends) of the congregation. It is possible for an instrumentalist to play a familiar hymn so meaningfully that hearts can be moved as effectively as if the words were sung. In my opinion, the latter approach is the only one valid in a worship service where corporate experiences are desired.

NON-CORPORATE INVOLVEMENT

As in organ music (see pp. 62–63), the instrumentalist may be called upon to provide an experience not tied to concrete ideas (text) in order that the members of the congregation can freely and creatively worship in their own individual directions. A prelude, offertory, or postlude normally functions that way, and the instrumentalist selects a piece that creates more abstract feelings and meanings, while being no less important and verifiable than textual meanings that are concrete. Such selections create the atmosphere within which the worshiper functions. In a sense that is what happens in instrumental concerts, but in service music the more abstract moods and feelings should tie in with a specific functional objective of the service. A quiet pastoral flute or oboe solo as part of a prelude can effectively focus on meditative, introspective, or serene moods and meanings as people are involved in preparation for worship. A joyful *allegro* from a Baroque sonata can function in a postlude as a joyous, dynamic experience creating a sense of direction and purpose as the worshiper leaves the sanctuary.

Whether for corporate or non-corporate involvement, it should be clear that:

- The instrumentalist must be guided in the selection chosen so that nothing is left to chance.
- The instrumentalist needs to play the selection in an appropriate performance style that reinforces the text or the appropriate abstract meanings; personal displays of virtuosity are out of place.
- Only selections that can function within the utilitarian context are acceptable; the instrumentalist is not playing *concert music*, but *service music* as a means to an end—to lead people in spiritual experience.

APPROPRIATE WRITTEN AND PERFORMANCE STYLES

So much of what is heard in church-related instrumental music today is approached only within the aesthetic context. Orchestral arrangements of hymns, whether symphonic or pop in nature, tend to divert the mind of the listener from the purpose of the piece (spiritual communication) to the pleasure motif (aesthetic gratification). Such elaborately recorded arrangements have obviously been conceived apart from the text and cater to the church public who often will not buy non-church orchestral literature but will buy "church tunes." Hearing a song Monday through Saturday misused as a pleasure-centered experience on Christian radio and then trying to sing or listen to the same tune on Sunday as a vehicle for worship may be confusing at best and, more likely, non-functional. Certainly reinforcement of basic textual ideas can take place in good orchestral settings, and not all recordings and Christian radio programs err in that regard. But often the average listener has difficulty making appropriate discriminatory judgments. Once again the vast amounts of music that are played primarily within an entertainment context on radio (although most stations desire to use their records in spiritual ministry) tend to lull the listener into thinking that whenever he hears church music its purpose is primarily aesthetic in nature. The questionable recordings are probably here to stay because the average Christian disc jockey is usually uninformed in such matters, but what is done in the church service can have such unmistakable focus that the worshiper will sense that it is different from listening to a radio station or recordings.

Whenever possible, it is advisable, especially in churches where instrumental music is misunderstood, to introduce the selection to be played verbally, focusing on the ideas to be conveyed. That may also be done in a short paragraph in the bulletin in place of a verbal statement. When the instrumental selection is used in non-corporate experience and when the congregation is aware of how to be effectively involved in such experience, nothing need be said. However, if that is not the case, the same educating responsibility exists here as in those moments when the organ functions as a vehicle for spiritual experience. Appropriate written and performance styles must be encouraged for service playing. Thus triple tonguing, "tearing all over" the piano, creating tonal approaches that are in themselves sensuous or more in keeping with the blues or other extra-spiritual experience, or any other instrumental technique that points more to the performer than the message is out of place. When any church musician by performance approach says, "Look at how good I am," one can be certain that such insincerity is inappropriate. What is needed is total congruity between the tonal approach, visual performance techniques, performance style, and the written style of the music.

7

The Involvement of Non-Musicians in the Church Music Program

THE CONGREGATION

The congregation is the most important group in the church music program since it is the purpose of all musicians and music groups to lead the congregation in active participation in the worship experience. In all services the congregation is never an audience for which musicians perform. It is, instead, the Body of Christ either actively participating in corporate and non-corporate God-directed worship experiences or else involved in a maturing process that ultimately issues in happy, healthy lives of service. The choir, organist, and minister of music all exist as leaders of the congregation. An anthem is sung as an expression of worship to God on behalf of the congregation as in other verbal corporate experiences. Anthems or songs of testimony or witness may be man-directed and legitimately communicate scriptural truth to fellow human beings, but in so doing they need to reflect honor and glory to the One of whom they sing.

THE PROBLEM OF NON-INVOLVEMENT

As was true prior to Martin Luther's revolutionary strategies, members of congregations of all denominations today may "check their brains at the door" upon entering the sanctuary and thoughtlessly go through the motions of the service. The problem of non-involvement is not a new one. In the medieval period "worshipers understood little of what was being said or sung, since the service was in Latin. Their own vocal participation was almost nil."* Although Luther loved the Latin setting of the mass, he recognized the need for the involvement of his worshipers in their own language. He therefore translated the Bible into German and used hymns as well as other specific portions of the service in the language of the people. Although his choir sang polyphonic settings in Latin, he had them help lead the congregation in the new homophonic settings of the chorales. Concerning the need for singing by the congregation, Luther wrote:

> The 96th Psalm [v. 1] says, "Sing to the Lord a new song. Sing to the Lord all the earth." For in the Old Covenant under the law of Moses, divine service was tedious and tiresome as the people had to offer so many and varied sacrifices of all they possessed, both in house and field. And since they were restive and selfish, they performed this service unwillingly. . . . Now with a heart as lazy and unwilling as this, nothing or nothing good can be sung. Heart and mind must be cheerful and willing if one is to sing. . . . Thus there is now in the New Testament a better service of God, of which the Psalm [96:1] here says: "Sing to the Lord a new song. Sing to the Lord all the earth." For God has cheered our hearts and minds through his dear Son, who he gave for us to redeem us from sin, death, and the devil. He who believes this earnestly cannot be quiet about it. But he must gladly and willingly sing and speak about it so that others may come and hear it.†

Luther's dilemma was probably greater than any that have existed since his time. Imagine a congregation that for years had functioned as spectators looking in on a mass that was generally void of personal subjectivity. Imagine being asked to *sing* in a new liturgical setting but not a new architectural setting. The mere idea of hearing one's own voice in such circumstances would be frightening. Luther had to choose tunes with which the people were familiar. The only place people sang was in the local pubs where the people socialized, caught up on the current news, and sang folk songs (sometimes with bawdy texts). Luther was smart enough to know he had to *start where the people were.*

*Donald P. Hustad, *Jubilate*, p. 107.
†Ulrich S. Leupold, ed., *Luther's Works*, vol. 53, pp. 332–33. Copyright © 1965 by Fortress Press. Used by permission.

As time passed, however, he recognized the incongruity of using tunes on Sunday mornings that were sung on Saturday night. He explicitly referred on several occasions in his writings to the paradox created by the mixture of associations caused by the singing of those tunes. In time, he corrected the problem by composing new tunes and also hiring other musicians to write original chorale melodies for the purpose of worship. He involved his people in the singing process through the use of pop tunes, but he moved on from that point as soon as he recognized the new problems thus created.

It is interesting how some current writers have used Luther to defend the use of pop styles today to encourage congregations to sing. However, Luther felt that great care needed to be taken to avoid using music that would detract from praising God. He stated:

> The subject is much too great for me briefly to describe all its benefits. *And you, my young friend, let this noble, wholesome, and cheerful creation of God be commended to you. By it you may escape shameful desires and bad company. At the same time you may by this creation accustom yourself to recognize and praise the Creator. Take special care to shun perverted minds who prostitute this lovely gift of nature and of art with their erotic rantings; and be quite assured that none but the devil goads them on to defy their very nature which would and should praise God its Maker with this gift, so that these bastards purloin the gift of God and use it to worship the foe of God, the enemy of nature and of this lovely art.**

To not tell the whole story of Luther's approach is either willful misrepresentation or shabby scholarship. Further, to liken the causes of non-singing congregations in the sophisticated twentieth century to Luther's situation reflects a whole series of problems in cause-and-effect evaluation and analytical techniques. To say that congregations and/or young people in particular do not sing because "they don't like the tunes" is only touching on the problem. Luther was probably close to the truth when he said that young people need

> something to wean them away from *love ballads and carnal songs* and to teach them something of value in their place, thus combining the good with the pleasing, as is proper for youth. Nor am I of the opinion that the gospel should destroy and blight all the arts, as some of the pseudo-religious claim. But I would like to see all the arts, especially music, used in the service of Him who gave and made them. . . . As it is, the world is too lax and indifferent about teaching and training the young for us to abet this trend.†

*Ibid., pp. 323–24, italics mine.
†Ibid., p. 316.

The *heart* of the problem is that people—young and old—have become conditioned to being spectators by the hours they spend watching television or sporting events. They think going to church is for something the church does for them as in watching television. Sadly, some pastors and church musicians are buying into that approach by, in fact, *doing* it for them. As mentioned in an earlier chapter, recorded orchestral tracks and some media-like techniques make services of worship into non-participatory spectator events. The cause of the problem is not bad music (although some, indeed, may be), but rather the lack of awareness of the purposes and procedures of the worship service itself. Many musicians who jumped on the pop music bandwagon a few years ago in order to better involve their congregations are now struggling with the non-involvement problem once again. It is difficult to keep up with all the new pop tunes so one can be "relevant" and keep the congregation involved.

Rather than solely focus on the music as the culprit that causes non-involvement it is better to focus on the responsibility of the worshiper, who must exert the effort to actively participate. The easy path is the one of accommodation. The best path is the one that has music suitable to the communication of scriptural truth. Assuming that non-involvement issues from a source other than an indifferent or non-existent relationship to God, a congregation can be taught how to worship. Again, classes or articles written for the church paper or bulletin can help a congregation learn that the act of singing in a worship service is not done for the pleasure of singing enjoyable tunes—sing-alongs and camp-sings serve that purpose. Service music is a vehicle for enhancing and supporting the meaning of the text and as such functions as a means to an end (spiritual involvement) rather than an end in itself (entertainment). Upon learning these perspectives, many churches are rediscovering the appropriateness and utilitarian solidity of the great hymns of the church for use alongside the functional and effective contemporary music of quality and significance. It is time for the church to challenge gifted composers to write church music that can evoke spiritual responses from people willing to give themselves to an active participation in services. Any new piece that can survive close scrutiny as to its appropriateness, both musically and textually, is worthy of use. If it does not measure up, why use it? The congregation deserves literature that is worthy of their time once they desire to become involved.

Leaders of worship often think that the only time people worship is when a singularly voiced audible experience takes place. Some of the most meaningful worship experiences can take place when members of the congregation creatively and individually worship the Lord, whether silently or aloud. For the congregation that has learned how to use time in that way, the time is well spent and may be a source of great meaning. It is important, then, that when such experiences are desired, the organist not play a familiar hymn encouraging minds to gravitate to the text, thus making the experience a corporate one (see pp. 62–63).

LITURGICAL VS. NON-LITURGICAL SERVICE SETTINGS

As a young man I was told by friends and relatives (as well as instructors in my early education) that liturgical churches are dead— they only go through the motions of worship and are lulled to sleep by the devastating effect of weekly repetitions. In later years I served as minister of music in five non-liturgical denominations and discovered the same lethargy and lack of involvement I had heard existed in only liturgical churches. Sitting on the platform or leading the congregational singing I could readily see the glassy eyes of people who were simply going through the motions. The order of worship (Prelude/Call to Worship/Invocation/Opening Hymn/Scripture Reading/Pastoral Prayer/Anthem/Announcements and Offertory—always with special music/Hymn/Sermon/Closing Hymn/Benediction/Postlude) had its own repetitive form that could tranquilize the congregation if they were at the mercy of forms to involve themselves. Orders of worship do not exist to interest or activate the congregation. Members of the congregation activate themselves to participate. The order of worship can meaningfully function if the people involve themselves. The forms are only a means to an end, never an end in themselves. Congregations may be involved or uninvolved in both liturgical and non-liturgical services. It is the task of church musicians to constantly encourage congregations to involve themselves regardless of the forms or styles of music used in churches.

There is no greater gratification for a minister of music than for a member of the congregation to say, "I profoundly worshiped today through the music" (unlike the comment "I *enjoyed* the music," which is like telling a pastor, "I *enjoyed* your sermon"). One should strive to provide experiences that evoke genuine and spiritually meaningful responses from all participants for the edification of the saints and the glory of God.

THE PASTOR-MINISTER OF MUSIC RELATIONSHIP

AS IT HAS BEEN

There probably is not a book written on this subject that does not stress the importance of the pastor's positive involvement in an effective church music ministry. However, it may be that some have over-stated the pastor's role. It is neither necessary nor ideal for the pastor to provide the primary leadership in the music life of the church. Undoubtedly the expected roles of the pastor in recent years have forced some clergy into a jack-of-all-trades involvement with a resulting master-of-none level of proficiency. Inadequate church budgets often hinder the work of the Lord although the pastor has the vision for a competent support staff.

But lack of money is not always the problem. Churches have required that pastors be psychologists in order to effectively counsel. They must be the equivalent of corporate presidents in order to run the complex administrative business affairs and budgetary matters of the church. Of course they must be sociologists, because it is impossible to relate to the social needs of people without such expertise. They certainly must be educators to teach the Word with a practical facility for current pedagogical techniques so as to effectively lead the church school program and possibly oversee an elementary, middle, and secondary school program associated with the church. If not a political activist, he must at least take positions on issues and possibly use the pulpit to articulate his own particular persuasion. If the pastor or church has aspirations for using the media (radio or television), he must be an effective salesman with the gift for raising money. Mannerisms, facial expressions, dress, and other personal characteristics must be developed in specific directions so as to make the package marketable. Some pastors and church musicians attend seminars that instruct in camera and staging techniques in order that services or programs to be aired appear professional. Finally, pastors are also expected to be good preachers.

Certainly many, perhaps all, of those expectations of the pastor have merit in one way or another. If the complex responsibilities of overseeing the music program of the church are added to the list, it becomes apparent that no one person can handle half of the assignments—much less all of them. And yet there are those who not only try to do some of the above but think they should. It is irrelevant to comment here on the effectiveness of the pastors who endeavor to be multi-faceted superpersons. It is evident that one-half or even one course in church music in seminary (as is the present requirement of many seminaries) will not begin to prepare the pastor in a thorough understanding of worship, hymnology, church music philosophy, and church music literature. It is no wonder that pastors are often admittedly confused or lacking in understanding in their leadership roles in church music.

Few pastors today deeply appreciate and understand the mission of music in the life of the church and have a vision of what ought to be in the utilization of the handmaiden of spiritual experience. Often their awareness encompasses only the records of their children, the old gospel songs of their youth, music of the media, Muzak they hear in the stores, and the few favorite hymns from their hymnbooks. The point is not to place blame on men of God called to the ministry but that the church expects an impossible breadth from pastors. Such demands have seriously diminished the effectiveness of many pastors in their primary tasks of being theologians, preachers, teachers of the Word, and godly ministers deeply committed to profound spiritual leadership through exemplary lives. Time demands made by all the peripheral responsibilities simply preclude the disciplined and exhaustive life of scholarship and study of the Word.

As the needs of the worshiper are considered, it would be far better to turn some of the responsibilities over to well prepared individuals and expect the pastor to concentrate upon the ministry of the Word. Much of what happens in church music today that is incongruous is the result of a hasty or ill-informed decision-making process by well-meaning pastors. When one has no clearly defensible reasons for objecting to inappropriate forms or styles as well as no vision as to what could be, expediency becomes the norm. The greater disservice to the church is the fact that the same pastors often rely on their church musicians for leadership, and they too are found wanting.

AS IT MIGHT BE

The ideal role of the pastor in church music is one where the pastor provides leadership in service objectives, mutually arrives at overall goals or objectives for the music program with the minister of music, and functions in the role of counselor to the minister of music. It should not be inferred that final authority does not rest with the pastor. The pastor is the shepherd of the flock and should have the ultimate influence in all important decisions. But the ideal situation is one in which pastor and minister of music function as a team with a sense of unity and purpose in implementation. That team relationship can only take place, however, when the following conditions exist:

- The pastor and minister of music understand and concur on basic theological and philosophical matters as they relate to the ministry of music; seminaries and graduate programs in church music must begin to provide better opportunities for the development of those competencies.
- Both individuals are capable and qualified in their own areas of specialization.

- The individuals complement each other in personal attributes and leadership style.
- Lines of communication are always kept open and regularly utilized; the climate of openness is nurtured so as to encourage the discussion of any matters of potential disagreement.
- Both individuals are secure in their own self-image so the effectiveness of each is no threat to the other but rather a reason for personal satisfaction.
- Each individual is openly supportive of the ministries of the other with an obvious awareness on the part of the laity that the relationship is not only a professional one but also one of love and singleness of purpose.

When one or more of the above do not exist, the ministry of both the pastor and the minister of music will be difficult. Tactful exchanges between the two parties can provide insight and increased awareness as to the individual points of view that can result in the above ideals. Of course, in-depth pre-employment interviews can avoid such a gulf before a minister of music is hired, but where there is a distinct gulf between the two, all effort must be made to resolve the problem. The Lord's work must not be allowed to suffer when dissension exists within the leadership ranks. If such problems exist, regardless of the cause, I believe the minister of music should open himself to another place of service. Because the pastor and minister of music must work so closely, and their responsibilities ideally interrelate, the pastor should initiate whatever action is necessary to guarantee a happy team relationship.

Occasionally a pastor may accept a call to a new ministry, leaving a good working relationship and supportive staff. It is my opinion that the minister of music (as well as other support staff) should be willing to resign if the new pastor has differing points of view. As coaches usually are free to bring their assistants with them or hire new assistants of their choice, so also is there wisdom in allowing a new pastor to build his own team. It is possible, of course, that the musician and new pastor will desire to be on the same team, but the door should be open for the pastor to select his own team members without embarrassment.

The ministry of music can be an experience of joy and productivity if the pastor-minister of music relationship is a good one. The call of God is essential for this to happen, and when it does, it is an exciting and challenging experience. What a privilege it is to serve God with a pastor whose signals are out of the same play book! It results in a deeply meaningful friendship and a happy situation in which to serve.

Perhaps the most important contribution a pastor can make to the total ministry of music in the church is his vocal support of the program and encouragement of those who participate. Where the pastor is dearly loved and respected because of his leadership in his other areas of responsibility, when he speaks in support of the ministry of music, such support helps insure effectiveness of the total program.

THE WORSHIP COMMITTEE-MINISTER OF MUSIC RELATIONSHIP

The worship committee has the potential of being a great asset or a major hindrance to the church music ministry. Where the committee is composed of members informed to some degree in matters of church music with an interest in assisting and supporting the church music program, the relationship can be positive. Conversely, where the committee is selected not on the basis of qualification but due to willingness to be on a committee, problems can arise. It becomes a primary task of the church musician to provide educational experiences for the committee so that they understand the basis of a sound church music program. Ideally where such committees exist the minister of music should first of all endeavor to tactfully and positively teach a series of classes for the committee and others in the church who may be interested. (I have found the Sunday school hour to be an effective time slot and in one church offered a thirteen-week course in church music. The course was popular enough for it to be re-offered several years in a row.) The minister of music should also work with the chairman of the nominating committee in order to have individuals on the worship committee who have the appropriate understandings. Nothing is more discouraging to a minister of music than to have a wonderfully functioning committee replaced by a whole new committee that requires a great deal of training.

The capable worship committee can function as a sounding board of the congregation, helping to avoid serious problems before they arise. Members can assist in routine matters such as making contacts, phone calls, recruitment of new members of groups, scheduling, and promoting of special events. In general, they can help interpret philosophical and theological implications of the program to the congregation. Obviously there can be a credibility gap between the minister of music and the committee if *either* is unqualified. Where tensions exist it is imperative that straightforward but loving and tactful verbal communication take place. In such instances examining and evaluating *ideas* rather than attacking people can solve problems. If the problem is due to a lack of qualification, seminars and formal courses can sometimes resolve the situation. Graduate programs for church musicians can often assist in upgrading the musician's expertise. Positive steps must always be taken to provide for growth and not allow problems to smolder beneath the surface. The Lord expects committee members and church musicians to have joy in their service for Him, and when such a relationship exists the focus of the efforts can then be on the primary area of importance—the involvement of the congregation in a meaningful spiritual experience through music.

PART 3

THE PROGRAM OF CHURCH MUSIC

8

Music Literature

When there are additional music staff members, the most important responsibility of the minister of music is to coordinate the music aspects of the services. As suggested earlier, all literature should be selected with the specific objectives of the service in mind. Each choir director should be free to select the literature for the choirs he conducts but should do so within the overall philosophical context of the music program. It is, of course, essential that music staff members be responsible to the minister of music so the program can have cohesiveness as the result of clearly understood philosophical and theological presuppositions.

Within those boundaries the staff should enjoy freedom in their own selection choices. Nothing is more stifling to a conductor than having to direct selections chosen by someone else. The key is to find capable team members and then give them freedom.

STAFF INVOLVEMENT

The choir director should choose anthems, calls to worship, and other responses sung by the choir. The organist selects the literature for the prelude, postlude, and the organ offertory. Ideally the pastor should select the hymns because he will best know the thrust of the service. Occasionally pastors aware of their hymnological inadequacies request that the minister of music select the hymns. In such instances a statement from the pastor indicating what is to be stressed in his sermon helps facilitate appropriate selections. Such advance communication not only keeps the pastor aware of the importance of appropriate hymn selections but supports the team relationship between the pastor and the music staff.

It is essential that all members of the staff who have anything to do with a worship service know well in advance what the theme of the service will be. Churches that follow a church calendar make advance planning easier for the music staff. In churches that set their own calendar it is essential that sermon topics and basic service objectives are planned well in advance to enable the music staff to choose literature that best supports the primary thrusts of the service. Perhaps one of the most difficult situations for the music staff is to work with a pastor who chooses his sermon topic one week prior to the Sunday on which it is preached. Choirs cannot give adequate preparation to anthems in support of such choices, organists cannot select literature well enough in advance to insure adequate practice, and in general, the service becomes a potpourri of events, all of which lack the unity necessary for effective worship. It is essential that the minister of music and other musicians have adequate time to select the literature to be performed with few last minute surprises.

QUALITATIVE FACTORS

Nothing can be worse than hearing a choir trying to sing anthems far too difficult for its level of achievement. Musicians bent on maintaining standards at all costs sometimes fail to realize they are sacrificing the standard of quality performance in order to try to reach some other standard. Certainly there is room and need for qualitative concerns in literature, but such concerns must be viewed within the context of the objectives of the service, the capabilities of the choir, and the musical and spiritual understandings of the congregation and the way in which music functions within the worship experience.

When a choir sings a good piece of music poorly, it not only renders the selection ineffective as a worship vehicle but also tends to set the minds of the people against that type of music in the future. The reason some people dislike the classics, for example, is that they have never heard a classical selection performed so well that the message could come through in all its power. Choirs that butcher Bach do a disservice to the congregation, the worship experience, the composer, and the Lord Himself. Bach or any other music should be performed only when the choir can so master the work that it can get out of the way of the piece and allow it to communicate effectively.

The highest levels of communication begin when technique is mastered. To talk communication without paying the price of technique mastery is shallow hypocrisy. The great "cop-out" is for musicians not to do their homework but simply assume the Holy Spirit will miraculously bless the performance. It is little wonder that many congregations dislike what could be a profoundly meaningful anthem for them.

The solution, of course, is to select good literature that is within the capabilities of the performer(s). Simple selections need not be trite. Hundreds of pieces are easy yet qualitatively good in music and text. The choir director must take the time necessary to find such selections. Occasionally literature clinics sponsored by publishers turn up a few good selections, but all too often they are pushing their newest releases, many of which do not pass the qualitative test. That may be the easiest way to find anthems but not necessarily the best way. If one is genuinely concerned about the quality of anthems chosen, the best approach is still the careful analysis of music and text.

MUSIC APPRECIATION

There is a sense in which minds and hearts are stretched a bit by hearing an anthem or the preaching of the Word. It is true that a congregation can grow in its appreciation and utilization of great literature if it is a subtle and non-confrontative effort. Worship services, however, are not classes in music appreciation. The service may educate spiritually but should not intentionally do so musically. All education efforts must therefore take place through appropriate classes and articles. It is no more defensible for people to believe that the thrust of a worship service is a music education experience than for them to believe it is entertainment or any other tangential objective. Services of worship and praise must be just that and nothing else. Those responsible must select the best literature possible that helps insure that such desired experiences will result. To select less than the best sells the Lord and the congregation short and suggests inadequate leadership.

All members of a congregation must be reached at some point in every service. That means that a service that only includes highly intellectual or esoteric materials will fly over the heads of a number of people in any given congregation. On the other hand, to insult the intelligence and understanding of another group in the same congregation by doing only simplistic materials is again a travesty. It therefore becomes necessary for the minister of music to coordinate the selection of literature so that there is the potential of reaching all who attend a service. Some writers in church music interpret that premise as requiring the selection of cheap, tawdry or musically sterile pieces. It is precisely because of the need to reach everybody that many churches include music that is profane in musical style. On the one hand, some churches are only concerned by the high standards that they can maintain in terms of literature selection; on the other hand some churches bend to the opposite extreme and include totally inappropriate selections. The point is that selections can be used that are simple in nature but qualitatively good. There is no need to compromise quality in order to reach everyone in the congregation.

My suspicion is that those who advocate the use of such literature do so with the underlying motivation of satisfying their own questionable musical needs rather than selecting literature that they know is uplifting and carries the spiritual potential for which people theoretically come to church. Where that problem occurs it is entirely possible it results as much from spiritual insensitivity and inadequacy as from poor musical judgment in literature selection.

ETHNIC LITERATURE

It is apparent that the Body of Christ is made up of as many cultures and subcultures as exist on the face of the earth. The beauty of the church in one sense is the ethnic diversity within the unifying centrality of Christ and His ministry in the lives of the members of the Body. Geographic location, language, social customs, historical background, and educational opportunities are all factors that weave strong threads in the total fabric of the church. As people differ so also are there valid differences in the way they worship and the music styles that reflect their understanding. Even within the same denomination in the United States, those in the South tend to approach the worship service somewhat differently from those in the North. West Coast churches tend to use some styles and approaches that differ from the Midwest or the East. The music used in the black church usually has significant characteristics that are unique to the religious experience of the black church.

Where practices reflect genuine ethnic or cultural considerations and are the product of the heritage of the people, there is legitimacy in the literature that is used. However, churches must be careful to not use the ethnic rationale as the catch-all that gives license to any extracultural practice. The basic values of Scripture (including the theological presuppositions of worship and the scriptural premise upon which worship is based) are absolutes that cut across all lines and ethnic origins. What is ethnically valid for one group of people by virtue of its heritage and experience may not be valid for another group that has not had similar experiences or heritage.

Ethnic variations are obvious and need not be defended. The my-approach-is-better-than-your-approach argument has never been viewed seriously by thoughtful believers, and the church can only be hurt by such proclamations. Rather, such differences are refreshing and reflect the kind of diversity that will be experienced someday in heaven.

There is a trend today to copy ethnic approaches because the imitators happen to *enjoy* the imitated style, or they may desire to identify with a specific ethnic group. One case in point is the trend of some white churches to use some of the gospel styles of the black church. Styles used in black churches are an outgrowth of the history of the black community. The context within which a black person sings is against the backdrop of slavery, discrimination, social injustice, and the bigotry that for years has marred this society. The black spiritual or gospel song becomes a release (as do many of the other aspects of the service) from the realities of life as they are. The hope of a better life in the future (or following death) is a primary theme. It is little wonder that black service music carries a high emotional content because of the hopeful possibilities of a better life.

For most white churches, imitating that approach is somewhat ludicrous, at best. To imitate poorly, as is usually the case, is only a kind of tokenism that reflects insincerity. Worse, some whites misuse the black styles because of the popularity of the style outside the church. To be sure, unique ethnic variations tend to blur within a melting pot society, and as one subculture appropriates values from another a good mix can result. But whites who have not truly suffered cannot internalize the meaning of a black style of music. At best it becomes a form of entertainment, a misuse of a style, and an insult to the black church. In our local community I have heard comments by blacks who strongly resent the imitation of whites who only do so for pleasure or aesthetic reasons.

Some styles are probably more accessible to the non-black community, and where such styles become genuinely meaningful, they are certainly valid. The concern, however, is that church choirs and soloists avoid using any literature because "it's fun to sing," or "audiences like it," or "it sells records," or "it's a good way to identify with the black community." All selections chosen for the service of worship and praise must have the potential of functioning effectively for the given congregation as vehicles for worship and praise. Again the criteria for selection must not be confused with those used in concert literature selection.

MUSIC FOR WEDDINGS AND FUNERALS

WEDDING MUSIC

Perhaps there is more misunderstanding in the realm of wedding music than in any other segment of church music. It seems likely that the misunderstandings relate more to the theological-philosophical intent of wedding services than to the actual music selection process itself. The secularization of church weddings is not uncommon, perhaps due to the fact that the institution of marriage itself is presently being challenged. Weddings are easily attainable through secular channels and often those that take place in the church reflect the looseness of commitment common to the easy marriage approach. Culturally, the attitude is that if it does not work it is easy to dissolve the marriage and try again. To the participants, subconsciously if not consciously, the wedding service then does not assume the import of a union made by God. Of course, music selected for a wedding is but a minor factor in the total picture but one that deserves careful consideration by those whose intent is to establish a Christ-centered home beginning with the vows and commitments made in the wedding itself.

A wedding is a sacred ceremony with many elements of a worship service included. The involvement of the bride, groom, and congregation in worship and praise of the Lord as well as the couple's involvement in the vows and prayers of commitment to each other and God are appropriate. If God is in fact joining them together, then the music used for the occasion must be scripturally based and musically appropriate. As in all church music there must be continuity and congruity of textual and musical meaning.

Although in one sense the wedding is a declaration of love between bride and groom, it is also a sacred commitment made before God and those gathered for the occasion. Every aspect of the service itself should be based upon scriptural principles and values. Therefore, in order that the music might be supportive and consistent, specific types of music are most appropriate. Secular love songs such as "Because," "I Love You Truly," "Love Theme from *Romeo and Juliet*," or other current popular love ballads, although they may be appropriate for some occasions, are not appropriate for the Christian wedding service. A number of quasi-religious pop songs written by current popular composers are presently being used in many church weddings and are also completely out of place. They may have the word God or church or some other reference to some aspect of Christianity included in the text, but by and large they are simply love songs. Songs of that nature abound in sentimentality and are used in some churches as traditional wedding music.

A number of writers in the church music field have pointed out that although the texts may indicate that a bride and groom are in love, such songs really are unnecessary inasmuch as they are saying what the bride and groom were supposed to have said to each other long before their marriage day. Certainly it must be assumed that a couple that is getting married is deeply in love. However, the wedding experience must be placed within the context of the Christian bride and groom's uniting their lives in sacred commitment to each other and God. It is thus a solemn occasion, one that demands the sincere involvement of the couple and of all who participate.

Therefore, good wedding music is not necessarily music that tells people how much in love the bride and groom are, but rather it should be music that reaffirms their commitment to Christ and their belief that marriage is a God-given institution needing God's blessing. Music with strong secular connotations, therefore, is not acceptable for wedding services. It should not be construed that the music need be of a somber or extremely serious mood. Joyous, happy, vibrant music that reflects the spirit of the occasion is most appropriate as long as it meets the basic criteria for the service. Hymn singing by the congregation is appropriate and should be given serious consideration by any couple planning a service. Thus wedding music and texts selected with the underlying thought of glorifying God should be suitable for a church service as distinguished from a social gathering.

When the couple wants to use a love song that they think of as "our song," or when they feel the need to share with their guests the fact that they are in love, the reception that often follows the wedding service would be a more appropriate occasion for such music. The less formal gathering provides an opportunity for socializing and receiving congratulations, as well as for the singing of songs that convey the joys and merits of love.

FUNERAL MUSIC

The funeral or memorial service for the believer is an occasion of grief and mourning but also one of great joy and confidence. Scripture does not say that the believers who remain following the loss of a loved one do not suffer great loss and mourn the death. Since grief is involved, it is appropriate that music be selected that has the capacity of providing comfort and spiritual encouragement. However, the blessed hope and joy of someday being united in heaven should also be expressed in the music for the funeral service. Many of the hymns of the church as well as certain of the gospel songs function most effectively in that regard. Favorite hymns of the departed are appropriate if requested by the family. Some of the most victorious experiences I have had have been in memorial services where the great truths of Scripture have been proclaimed through song, and the victory of the believer in life after death is joyfully and heartily sung by the congregation.

Ministers of music have probably all had experiences when there have been rather strange requests made. On one occasion I heard of an individual who requested "Tiptoe Through the Tulips" to be sung at his funeral. In such instances the minister of music or organist can tenderly and tactfully steer the family in directions of better appropriateness with the intent of ministering to the needs of all who will be in attendance.

Weddings and funerals should not be occasions for the display of great talents or artistic exhibitions. In both instances the occasions are ones that should most deeply reflect the spiritual commitment and spiritual dimensions of lives to be lived or lives that have been lived in honor and praise of God. The thrust, then, is to honor and glorify God above all else and bear witness to a commitment to Him and His Word. Once again the music will be appropriate when it effectively leads the congregation in spiritual experience and focuses primarily on the worship and praise of the Lord God.

EVALUATION OF CHURCH MUSIC

Some writers in the church music field prefer to avoid evaluating church music quality in any way other than the context of utilitarian effectiveness. Certainly that is a major concern and one that needs honest and careful scrutiny. The purpose of church music is, after all, to be the vehicle of spiritual communication as a means rather than an end. If it does not function effectively in that regard its validity can be seriously questioned.

When evaluating a non-art instrument pragmatically it is reasonable to evaluate only function. If an escalator does not effectively carry people from one floor to the next, its value is questionable. If the dishwasher does not effectively wash the dishes, it is worthless. However, when art, which can be evaluated within an aesthetic context, is appropriated to function primarily in a utilitarian context, the art form does not lose its total identity with the aesthetic realm. New buildings may be constructed primarily for utilitarian purposes, but they are also evaluated as to their aesthetic quality. Hideous architecture may function effectively but it is still hideous architecture. How much better it is to have architecture that functions effectively and is also pleasing to the eye! Regardless of how much one may argue for evaluation based solely on function, when art forms are involved, aspects of form, structure and beauty are bound to be part of the evaluative procedure.

In one of the most important books in the field of music education, *Foundations and Principles of Music Education*, authors Charles Leonhard and Robert W. House state:

> Almost everyone proceeds on the assumption that music varies in quality, that some music is better than other, that one composition is superior to another. This assumption is borne out by the fact that some musical compositions have gained and maintained a place in the permanent repertory while others, although they may achieve singular popularity for a time, are soon forgotten and revived only for their historical interest. It is also true that some music affects listeners and gives them pleasure while other music lacks appeal and leaves listeners unaffected. Thus music does vary in quality.*

Music can be categorized as bad, good, and great. The *good* category is described as:

- Music that is expressive in that it embodies the composer's conception of the stress-release (struggle-fulfillment) form of human experience
- Music that is put together with expert craftsmanship
- Music in which one musical element usually receives predominant emphasis (strong melodic, harmonic, or rhythmic content)
- Music that is usually less abstract in meaning

Great music, in addition to the first two points above, is music that:

- Is more subtle in expression
- Tends toward less concrete levels of meaning and more toward the abstract
- Has balanced emphasis in melodic, harmonic, and rhythmic content
- Expresses symbolically the life of feeling that transcends language or other common forms of human expression†

Music that does not fit into either of the above categories is questionable music and may be bad art. It is apparent that there can be

---

*Charles Leonhard and Robert W. House, *Foundations and Principles of Music Education*, p. 101.
†Ibid., pp. 102–7.

good or bad music in many different styles, including hymns, folk songs, pop, jazz, anthems, and symphonies. Although fewer in number, some selections within those same categories can also be considered great.

The concern here is that the church musician not abdicate the responsibility of total evaluation—both utilitarian and aesthetic—when selecting literature. Those who dismiss the concern for good quality in church music do so either out of ignorance or for personal benefits. If one can divert people's attention from qualitative concerns, then one can sell literature that would not otherwise pass the test. Such "cheap" literature fades quickly and must be replaced with more literature, thus figuring into the marketing schemes of some companies. Good or great literature has lasting quality and may remain part of the church experience for many years. Without sacrificing utilitarian priorities, the church musician owes the Lord the best in art that will also function effectively within the specific church context.

9

Graded Choirs and Instrumental Ensembles

SINGING: A SERIOUS BUSINESS

It is essential that the church provide opportunities for members of the congregation to develop and utilize their talents in praise of God. With budgeting cutbacks in music education throughout the nation the church graded choir program can do much to fill the vacuum created by abdication in the public schools. One of the best ways to involve children in the work of the Lord is through the choir program. If the choirs are directed by capable musicians who are spiritually mature, great benefits can accrue to the participants and the church. Obviously, the adult singers of tomorrow are in the youth choirs of today.

The leadership of the choirs must be carefully chosen. A full-time minister of music who is qualified may be responsible for directing all groups. However, there are often those in the congregation who may be particularly qualified to work with children or who may in fact be specialists in working with specific age groups. Few ministers of music are equally capable of working with all age levels. Thus a program can often benefit from using several directors where resources so allow. The minister of music then coordinates the program and guides the music staff toward the agreed upon goals.

Ideally, each choir should be involved in at least one of the services monthly. Choirs need to sing in public for adequate growth to take place. Singing too often will result in lack of preparation and confidence, and singing too seldom will result in motivational problems. Pieces chosen must be as thoughtfully selected as the literature for the main adult choir. It is important that the children's choirs not just sing fun songs but solid pieces that can be understood by the children and that also convey spiritual truth appropriate to the service in which they sing.

If there is a single problem in the youth choir movement today it is the underestimation of what children are capable of musically and spiritually. In a good school system children are taught sophisticated concepts and advanced thought patterns in math and science classes. In some schools, sadly, the arts are often relegated to a backseat and become a fun-and-games involvement or deviation experience that gives release from the other important "solid" course requirements. When those same young people go to their church choir, unfortunately, the same fun-and-games approach may be followed. Selected pieces are often void of both spiritual and musical content.

Sometimes the excuse given for such approaches is that it keeps the young people coming by not being too serious. In essence, such an approach by implication teaches young people that singing in a youth choir is not a serious business and perpetuates the myth that worship and praise experiences are made up of musical elements that are trite, unchallenging, and only entertaining. Publishers have bombarded the scene with musicals and other materials to accommodate such approaches. Contrary to what some think, churches that approach the graded choir program seriously, using quality literature and employing talented directors, have little problem in filling the rows of their choirs. I am aware of a number of churches where literature of high quality is used and large numbers of young people are meaningfully involved. In fact, children from other churches are often enrolled in those programs because home churches provide only surface experiences. The key is that the choir members are fully aware that they lead in a serious and important spiritual ministry that requires the best of literature and effort.

DISCIPLINE AND ACHIEVEMENT

In conveying the seriousness of serving the Lord it is important that the rehearsals reflect a good level of personal as well as technical choral discipline. Never should children be taught by implication or experience that serving the Lord is an act of insincerity. It can be argued that certain of the musicals carry basic scriptural truths and teach narratives of Scripture vividly. However, some of those musicals are basically cute, pop arrangements and in essence teach the children that youth choir programs are essentially shallow experiences. Obviously, children's choirs can only achieve their potential if the leadership is capable. Many church programs suffer from poor leadership—not by design but because competent trained leadership is not available. The joy of serving Christ is only fully realized when great effort is made and the results are above the level of the mundane and profane.

Small churches should not be exempt from including youth choirs in the music program. Grouped according to age, eight or ten youngsters can be the beginning of a choir. If the group is smaller it can be called an ensemble. The key is to select literature within the grasp of the group but not beneath them. Regular weekly rehearsals with basic attendance requirements are essential. Good literature appropriate to small group performance is available. Again, where only little commercial, jingle-like tunes are used, the children grow up with no hymnological heritage to treasure. As long as the truth of the texts can be taught so that they understand what they sing, hymns are a good source for materials, as well as being a valuable experience for the singers. Young people whose basic church music diet is "Christian contemporary" are sold short. Through no fault of their own they are deprived of experiences in theology and doctrine that help sustain the believer in later life.

There are a number of good patterns upon which to base a graded choir program. Each church should select the organizational approach that fits its own specific situation. Ideally, a program should be structured so as to provide opportunities for all children of public school age. One usable organizational arrangement is as follows:

- *Cherub Choir:* girls and boys kindergarten through second grade
- *Chapel Choir:* girls grades three through five
- *Sanctuary Choir:* girls grades six through eight
- *Boys Choir:* boys grades three through eight (or when voice changes)
- *Cathedral Choir:* girls and boys grades nine through twelve
- *Senior Choir:* adults—college to retirement age
- *Festival Choir:* adults—college and older (open without audition to anyone who would like to sing)

The grade intervals from choir to choir may vary from one church to the next. Good reasons can be given for several different breakdowns. Some churches also include a senior citizens choir, which has enormous merit. In addition to singing in services that group can sing at hospitals and nursing homes, go caroling at Christmas, and assist in other aspects of the church program. It provides a much needed opportunity for seniors to continue to feel that they can serve God and make an important contribution to the life of the church. Individually they also benefit greatly from the fellowship and social experiences.

Throughout any graded choir program, musicianship, vocal techniques, music reading, and music appreciation should be taught. However, the primary purpose of any church group is not to become great performers or proficient musicians but leaders in spiritual experiences through the vehicle of music. Techniques and competencies must always be taught as a means to eventual effective communication. It is true that church musicians are charged with the responsibility of assisting all of the members of the church in developing whatever gifts God has given them. A major part of that responsibility is carried out through the graded choir program. One must not lose sight of the fact that the difference between church and non-church musicians is that church musicians use music as a means to an end rather than as an end in itself. The focus of all learning experiences is to develop and use one's talents to serve and glorify God.

HANDBELL CHOIRS

Handbell choirs are perhaps the fastest growing musical movement in churches in the United States today. Some churches have an equivalent handbell choir for every choral group in the church. Good literature has become available, and the beauty the bells add to preludes, offertories, and anthems makes contributions by bell choirs most welcome. Qualified leaders are necessary in this as in any other program so that techniques of ringing and musicianship can be taught to insure growth and success. Unique combinations of ringers such as family bell choirs (made up of two or three families), senior citizens' bell ringers, or boys who prefer not to sing in the singing choirs all provide special opportunities for musical involvement in the church. As with the other music organizations, the bell choirs need to be scheduled on a regular basis into the service calendar. The portability of the instruments makes it possible for these choirs to play in various church locations as well as outside the church service context. Small and large churches alike find the contributions of bell choirs to be beautiful and spiritually rewarding.

INSTRUMENTAL ENSEMBLES

Instrumental groups can serve a useful purpose in the church program in a number of ways. Instruments can play for congregational singing and in so doing enhance the worship and praise experience. Instrumental groups may accompany cantatas or major works in concerts or services. They can also be used to play preludes, postludes, and offertories as well as to accompany soloists in services. Finally, instrumental groups provide talent maturation opportunities for instrumentalists in the church.

Churches located in areas where there are good school orchestra and band programs may find that the school programs are so demanding that it is difficult to sustain a church program. However, a church program that only offers vocal opportunities cheats those in the congregation who are instrumentalists. Ideally, the church will provide instrumental opportunities if it intends to offer a balanced program with a potential involvement of all instrumentalists in the congregation.

As with other music programs in the church, the purpose of instrumental music is to lead the church in a spiritual experience. Concerts can be a valid part of the program but most important is the instrumental ensembles' unique involvement in the services of the church. In the selection of literature the criteria for appropriateness is the same as that for the instrumental soloist and the organist. As instrumentalists become involved in the church music program the ultimate goal should be the development of a band and/or orchestra. Again, as the music programs of public education are cut back, the possibilities for the development of a band or orchestra in the church increase. Perhaps the time is near when more and more churches will experience the thrill of the ancient description of the lifting up of voices and instruments in praise of God found in 2 Chronicles 5:13–14:

> It came . . . to pass, as the trumpeters and singers were as one, to make one sound to be heard in praising and thanking the Lord; and when they lifted up their voice with the trumpets and cymbals and instruments of music, and praised the Lord, saying, For he is good; for his mercy endureth for ever: that then the house was filled with a cloud, even the house of the Lord; so that the priests could not stand to minister by reason of the cloud: for the glory of the Lord had filled the house of God.

10

The Music Program in the Small Church

It could be concluded that the perspectives of this book practically apply only to large churches with ideal budgets. It is true that smaller churches often have music programs that are less than what they should be, but this is most often due to a lack of vision and philosophic commitment rather than size. Considering that at least 50 percent of the time spent in most services is spent in music experiences, it is a short-sighted pastor and/or church that opts for a minimal music ministry.

Some churches would rather limp along with unpaid, incompetent music leadership than adequately fund salaries and the purchase of much needed literature. Competent church musicians cannot usually contribute their services when music is an integral part of their professional life (any more than a pastor can contribute his services free of charge). The education of a musician is (next to that of a physician) the most expensive education to earn. Private lessons alone are very costly, and the musician is forced in normal circumstances to recover some of those costs through salaries. Because church musicians are salaried does not in any way detract from the fact that they can be and must be dedicated servants of the Lord. It simply boils down to the fact that musicians must pay their bills like everyone else. In a sense, churches can well expect that what they invest in the music program will or should provide rich dividends for the congregation and the various ministries of the church as a whole.

Many churches with memberships of 150 have music ministries that are exemplary and easily support the basic tenets of this book. Theological, philosophical, psychological, and musical points of view can all be pragmatically embraced by the minister of music and pastor in the small church. Very often excellent programs are led by part-time musicians who have demonstrated strong music and leadership abilities. The small church must be careful to not be handicapped by full or part-time leadership that is incompetent. *The key to an effective music ministry is not necessarily in developing a large budget but in employing capable leadership.* Young musicians are increasingly becoming available for careers in church music, and the future is bright for churches that have the appropriate vision. It would be hard to ascertain whether or not there is a cause and effect relationship, but it has been my experience that vital churches large and small all have vital music ministries.

In the small church the pastor usually has to assume a wide range of responsibilities, including the music program. Although in a small church with eighty-seven members there may not be a choir as such, very often there are those in the congregation who have talent and can voluntarily assist in music leadership. A mixed quartet, octet, or ensemble can provide excellent leadership in congregational singing or in leading in worship through an anthem. In those churches, the members are often reticent to initiate their involvement in music leadership because the pastor is usually the initiator. The fact is that most pastors appreciate the voluntary involvement of talented members. Ten percent of the average service attendance is a valid approximation of the number of people ideally involved in the music ministry. Therefore, it is reasonable that eight or nine people in a church of eighty-seven could have some basic music gifts. In a church of three hundred, a reasonable goal is thirty in the choir.

Perhaps the most important counsel that can be given the small church is one of encouragement toward growth that is not necessarily numerical in nature. Small churches can send their musicians to church music workshops and seminars just as large churches do. The increased insight and vision of those experiences can often ignite the flame of spiritual growth in the smallest of churches. Rather than look longingly at other church programs, we should recognize that the Lord expects the best from His people where He has put them to serve.

The important questions in church music do not focus on how many staff members are in a church or how large the budget might be. The questions of importance all focus on whether or not music experiences are being regularly used to enter the presence of God Almighty to express adoration, love, and praise and to proclaim Him worthy of worship. Such devotion can happen in small churches as readily as in large.

11

The Challenge of Tomorrow's Church Music Program

Attitudes in church work that foster mediocrity are the biggest contributors to continuing mediocre performance of church music and must be eliminated. Particularly in the realm of *church* music, it is incongruous for a musician to give less than his best for his Lord. It is imperative that he do his best work, not only to achieve at a high artistic level—like secular artists—but also because of a higher spiritual calling to honor God to the maximum. Pastors, ministers of music, or anyone else in charge of hiring or arranging for performing personnel should not only know the difference between mediocre and outstanding performance but should also have a willingness to maintain and support those who are outstanding performers. The challenge to Christian higher education in that regard is to produce outstanding young musicians who are committed to Christ and willing to give of their very best in service to Him. All too often churches desire the best, but dedicated musicians are not available. It is imperative that those institutions charged with the responsibility of producing church musicians do so with that qualitative concern in mind. The future for well-educated, talented church musicians has never been brighter.

Perhaps today as never before the church has the opportunity of assuming the leadership role in the music education of its members. The public sector is struggling to keep the arts alive in school. In some areas of the country where music educators have capitulated to the pressures of stressing current pop styles in the curriculum there is little reason for funding such music programs. Music teachers bent on being "with it" with their students spend precious class and rehearsal time perfecting the same tunes the young people do on their own. Public school rock groups and swing choirs are fine when they are a reasonable part of a balanced music education experience. But when they become the backbone of the program it is little wonder that budgets are cut. A principal told me recently that he seriously questioned any school system that funded programs that in fact do not educate. He said, "The young people come into class loving 'their' music and leave with nothing more than when they came in." If disciplines such as math, science, or social studies were involved in teaching young people what they already know, such programs would also be challenged. It is therefore little wonder that music teachers in the public sector are now re-evaluating their own positions. Only those programs with substance will survive. In the meantime the church can step in and fill the void. If it does not, Christian young people will be deprived of the opportunity to develop their music talents.

Churches throughout the United States are hiring full-time qualified musicians as ministers of music to provide the leadership for full-scaled music programs. Churches no larger than three hundred members are planning programs including music schools that offer private lessons in piano, organ, voice, guitar, and band and orchestra instruments. History shows that when the public sector does not meet the needs of its constituency in the arts, the church will step in and fill the gap.* The opportunity the public sector is neglecting in music education can become a great opportunity for the church. Properly conceived, expanding church music ministries can result in great spiritual growth in tomorrow's church.

The challenge to today's forward-looking church is to make it possible for young and old to develop and utilize their God-given talents

---

*See chapter 3 "Historical Foundations of Music Education," in Charles Leonhard and Robert W. House's *Foundations and Principles of Music Education,* McGraw-Hill, pages 45–81. This chapter gives an excellent historical sketch of music education and those points in history when the church was actively involved in music education. In California, where there have been considerable cutbacks in music in the public schools, many churches have added comprehensive music education programs. Small community churches as well as larger churches are offering choir and handbell courses, music theory and appreciation courses, as well as private lessons in instruments and voice.

in the church. Creative members of the congregation should be encouraged to develop that creativity within the context of a scriptural framework with the appropriate accompanying spiritual values. It is not only exciting but staggering to see what can happen to the worship service if the church has a support program supplying musicians to lead in the worship of God. Talented young people who once thought they would become public school music educators are now seriously pursuing the possibility of using their talents in full-time music ministry in the church. Churches with a vision in that regard are encouraging their young musicians in composition and assisting with scholarships for collegiate study. Graduate programs are being developed to assist young people in becoming musically competent and deeply committed servants whose gifts can be utilized fully in the church.

As the great church musician Bach wrote at the top of his manuscripts, "Jesus, help me!" and at the end of each score, "Solely to the glory of God," so also should the music program of every church where the gospel is preached seek the assistance and glory of God Almighty.

> O all ye powers that He implanted
> Arise, keep silence now no more;
> Put forth the strength that God has granted!
> Your noblest work is to adore!
> O soul and body, join to raise
> With heartfelt joy our Maker's praise.*
> (Johann Mentzer)

Bibliography

Dinwiddie, Richard. "Money Changers in the Church." *Christianity Today*, 26 June 1981.

Hustad, Donald P. *Jubilate*. Carol Stream, Ill.: Hope Publishing, 1981.

Leonhard, Charles, and House, Robert W. *Foundations and Principles of Music Education*. 2d ed. New York: McGraw-Hill, 1972.

Leopold, Ulrich S. *Luther's Works*, vol. 53. Philadelphia: Fortress, 1965.

Lovelace, Austin C., and Rice, William C. *Music and Worship in the Church*. Nashville: Abingdon, 1976.

Meyer, Leonard B. *Music, the Arts and Ideas*. Chicago: U. of Chicago, 1967.

"Resisting the Tide." *Eternity Magazine*, July 1971.

Robertson, James D. "The Nature of Christian Worship." *Asbury Seminarian* 2 (1953):28.

Routley, Erik. *Words, Music and the Church*. Nashville: Abingdon, 1968.

Schalk, Carl. *Church Music and the Christian Faith*. Carol Stream, Ill.: Agape Publishing, 1978.

————. *Key Words in Church Music*. St. Louis: Concordia, 1978.

Moody Press, a ministry of the Moody Bible Institute, is designed for education, evangelization, and edification. If we may assist you in knowing more about Christ and the Christian life, please write us without obligation: Moody Press, c/o MLM, Chicago, Illinois 60610.